D0857844

A
CENTURY
OF
TRIBUNE
EDITORIALS

A
CENTURY
OF
TRIBUNE
EDITORIALS

Essay Index Reprint Series

BOOKS FOR LIBRARIES PRESS
FREEPORT, NEW YORK

STANDARD BOOK NUMBER:

8369-1558-5

LIBRARY OF CONGRESS CATALOG CARD NUMBER:

72-93327

PRINTED IN THE UNITED STATES OF AMERICA

FOREWORD

Editorials are not written for posterity. No man, sitting down to write one, says to himself: "I shall now commit to paper a few thoughts so profound, so penetrating, so happily expressed, that the day must come when these words of mine will be lifted from the dust of the files to find immortality within the covers of a book." Editorials are written of and for the day of publication.

Nevertheless, here is the book and a few explanations are in order. The occasion for it is, of course, the centennial of THE TRIBUNE's founding on June 10, 1847. To mark the event, three volumes of Mr. Philip Kinsley's historical survey of the paper have been published and a fourth is in preparation. A detailed index of the newspaper from its earliest days is also under way and will be made available to historical libraries along with a complete filming of the files.

Those are exhaustive works. No comparable claim can be made for this book. It consists of 100 editorials (what other number would have been appropriate?) chosen from among the 150,000 or so that THE TRIBUNE has published in the course of a century. Those selected are not "the hundred best," no matter how *best* may be defined. They were chosen with a rather diffuse aim: some because they influenced events; some because they furnish a contemporary view of great men and great crises; some for their perception of things to come; a few for their quaintness and a few more for the quality of their writing. At least one was included for its egregiously bad writing. Because this is a birthday book, a fair number of the editorials deal with THE TRIBUNE itself; the birthday child is thus allowed to tell in his own words about himself and his moral and material progress at various stages in his career.

There is a good deal in the book that may prove of value to students of political, social, or economic history, and students of journalism will find material here bearing on the developing technique of editorial writing. In making the selections, those interests were never wholly forgotten, but, in general, the aim was to disclose the mind of THE TRIBUNE and the strategy of its editorial page from time to time as the century advanced. These readings in institutional growth, it was thought, would be welcomed by many of the friends of the newspaper and, possibly, even by some of its ill-wishers.

No attempt has been made, in selecting the material, to show that THE TRIBUNE has been consistent in its views and attitudes. Even a casual perusal will disclose deviations and contradictions and a close examination will discover a good many of them, the inevitable consequences of changing personnel, changing times and a longer perspective. Whether a consistent thread of political and moral principle can be traced in the book is for the reader to decide.

There can be no doubt, however, that the literary form of the editorial underwent a good many changes in the century. Today we are less oratorical, more colloquial. The thoughts of the youth of this newspaper were, in the main, long, long thoughts. Sentences went on and on. Paragraphs filled half a column. Punctuation was overdone, with a profusion of dashes, commas, and semi-colons where the need for them is not apparent, at least to the modern reader. Many words like *Slave* were introduced generally with a capital letter, for what reason we do not know, and some proper nouns were not similarly dignified.

We have left the sentences about as they were, including grammatical errors, and have made only a few deliberate changes in spelling and punctuation to correct obvious misprints. The capitals were retained in all their splendor except that the old custom of printing men's names in small capitals was dropped to avoid a confusing emphasis. It is difficult for a present-day copyist to follow the older fashions and probably some modernizations have crept in. They should not be numerous, however. In this sense, the book will serve as a museum of changing newspaper practice.

The longest paragraphs in some of the earlier editorials have been broken up to let in a little typographic light and air. That seemed to be the thing to do, but the task was not at all easy and the results have not always been fortunate. Those monumental paragraphs were found, on examination, to have a beginning, a middle, and an end; they were immense, but they had the integrity of an elephant and his dignity, too. Maybe they should have been left intact.

An obvious fault in the book is its lack of chronological balance. It is overloaded with editorials from some of the early and late periods, with the result that the middle decades are relatively neglected. This defect would have been avoided if the first plan to suggest itself—one year, one editorial—had been followed. That scheme was abandoned, however, partly because a few of the early volumes were lost in the great fire of '71 and, despite persistent effort, have never been replaced; and more particularly because the method would have permitted only the most inadequate showing of the characteristic ways in which the newspaper has deployed its forces for attack and defense.

The first decade is wholly unrepresented. The reason is that Joseph Medill and his colleagues did not take over the paper until 1855 and only then did the institution we now know have its true beginnings. A few years later, the controversy aroused by the decision in the Dred Scott case found THE TRIBUNE conscious of its mission, and with its character and method well established. Accordingly, the first item in the book is the editorial from 1857, interpreting the court's finding.

Each editorial in the collection is preceded by a brief note in italics, intended to sketch the historical setting, to suggest why the piece was included, or to tell how it all turned out. A footnote here and there may help to illuminate more or less obscure references in the text to such matters as the Black Laws of Illinois or to such worthies as Maj. Gen. Twiggs. As our own times are approached, the notes all but disappear, for this book, like the editorials of which it is composed, was designed for its day and not for posterity.

The editor of Volume Two of readings from THE TRIBUNE's editorial pages (to be published a hundred years from now) thus gets no help from us in discovering what the initials in NRA signify. In solving his puzzles, it is most unlikely that he will find assistance more alert than that provided for the present book by Mr. Smutny, Mr. Bradfield, Mr. Garrett, and especially Mrs. Cullen of THE TRIBUNE's research staff. Certainly the editor of 2047 will be most fortunate if he is guided in gathering his material by two such devoted searchers of the files as Mr. Philip Kinsley and Mr. Carl Wiegman, and if he has the moral equivalent of a Mr. Reuben Cahn and a Mr. William Cessna at hand to call attention to omissions. To all of these colleagues and to Mr. Malcolm Little who shepherded the book through the press and offered many valuable suggestions, your editor, secure in the anonymity that goes with his calling, is deeply indebted.

Tribune Tower
March 10, 1947

TABLE OF CONTENTS

A CENTURY

OF

TRIBUNE EDITORIALS

ILLINOIS NO LONGER A FREE STATE

May 16, 1857

Chief Justice Taney announced the decision in the Dred Scott case on March 6, 1857.

Is Illinois a Free State? She was one up to March 6th, 1857. On that day the five Slave-holders and one dough-face of the United States Supreme Court, constituting a majority of the National Tribunal, solemnly decided:

First—That black men, whose ancestors came from Africa, were not and could not be citizens of the United States.

Second—That black men *had no rights* which white men were bound to respect.

Third—That black men, whose ancestors were brought to this country as slaves, are *property*, exactly the same as oxen or sheep.

Fourth—That the Constitution of the United States recognizes *slaves as property*, and makes no difference whatever between them and horses, wagons, and any other kind of property.

From these premises the Court laid down the law that a Slave-holder has the *same right* to take and hold Slaves in any Territory, that he has to take and hold horses; and that he cannot be deprived of the right to hold Slaves in the Territories, any more than of the right to hold his horses and farming utensils.

We may reply that it is a bad law; that it is a false interpretation of the Constitution; that it does not repre-

DOUGHFACE: an easy political convert, especially a northern adherent of southern political principles.

sent the judicial or legal opinion of the nation. So have Judges McLean and Curtis replied; but the five Slave-holders and one doughface have over-ruled their opinion, as well as every other man's and settled the law. It is the final action of the National Judiciary, established by the founders of the Republic, to interpret the Constitution.

The Court has only *applied* its decision to the Territories, but if the new doctrine applies to Territories it must apply with equal force to the States. No State has the constitutional or legal right to prevent the citizens of another State from bringing their horses, cows or furniture within its jurisdiction, and having brought them from holding or using them; and it is by virtue of the Constitution that the emigrant from one State into another possesses these rights of property. Now, if the Constitution of the United States recognizes Slaves as property, differing in no respect, as the Supreme Court declares, from any other property, then no State Court, Legislature or State Constitution can deprive the owner of such slave property of the full use and enjoyment of it in any State into which he may see proper to emigrate with his negroes.

Under this decision, Douglas may bring his plantation negroes, in North Carolina and Mississippi, into Illinois, and set them to farming his lands in this State, with the Editor of the Chicago *Times* for his overseer, and no law of the State of Illinois can interfere to prevent him. We really can see nothing in the law, as interpreted by Taney & Co., to prevent opening a Slave pen and an auction block for the sale of black men, women and children right here in Chicago. And if there is any doubt on the subject, the forthcoming decision on the Lemmon case will remove it. Slavery is now national. Freedom has no local habitation nor abiding place save in the hearts of Freemen. Illinois in law, *has ceased to be a free State!*

THE LEMMON CASE: In 1852, Jonathan and Juliet Lemmon, Virginians, took eight slaves with them to New York to await a ship bound for Texas where the Lemmons intended to settle. In a habeas corpus proceeding, the slaves were declared to be free. There was great indignation in the south and the attorney general of Virginia was authorized by his state's legislature to intervene in the appeal. He, of course, argued that the Dred Scott precedent was binding. A decision upholding the lower court was handed down, however, in December, 1857, seven months after the editorial appeared. A second appeal, this time to New York's highest court, was decided in 1860 and was also favorable to the Negroes.

A QUESTION OF TASTE
July 22, 1858

The Democrats had nominated Douglas for re-election to the United States senate. Lincoln was his Republican opponent. Greeley in New York and others had proposed a formal debate between these champions. Lincoln was more than willing, but Douglas hesitated, so the tradition goes, until stung into acceptance by THE TRIBUNE'S *taunt.*

It is no doubt distasteful in a high degree to Senator Douglas and those people who are interested for him, that there is any such person in the State of Illinois as Abraham Lincoln. It is evident, also, from the columns of the Chicago *Times* that Mr. Lincoln's room is preferred to his company whenever there is any speaking to be done or any lies to

be told. Mr. Douglas' words turn to ashes in his mouth whenever he spies out his antagonist in his audience. Every Douglasite in the State feels as though he had bitten a green persimmon when Mr. Lincoln's presence is announced in their midst. He operates on their nerves like a detective officer. They deem it evidence of exceeding bad taste that he should ever happen to be in their neighborhood at all. "Mr. Douglas does not mind it," says the *Times.* O, of course not; he rather likes it. But his organist finds it worth while to devote two-thirds of a column to an essay on the vulgarity displayed by Mr. L. in that connection.

We have a suggestion to make which will perhaps help the *Times* out of its difficulty. Let Mr. Douglas and Mr. Lincoln agree to canvass the State together, in the usual western style. We have reason to believe this would meet Mr. Lincoln's views. In this way the people can make up their minds as to which candidate is right. If Mr. Douglas shall refuse to be a party to such arrangement, it will be because he is a coward. We are well aware that so long as he accomplishes his purpose, he cares not how he accomplishes it. But he must either go with Mr. Lincoln now, or run away from him as he did in 1854. Which will he do?

WHY DOUGLAS DUCKS AND DODGES
August 30, 1858

The first of the Lincoln-Douglas debates took place at Ottawa, on Aug.

4

21, 1858. The seventh and last meeting was at Alton on Oct. 15.

The purpose here, as in a number of other editorials published while the debate was in progress, was to exploit a particular weakness in the Douglas position.

On the 16th day of June, 1858, the Republican party of Illinois at Springfield, through its 1,000 delegates from ninety-eight counties, adopted a platform of principles. It then and there nominated Abraham Lincoln as its candidate for United States Senator, and placed him upon said platform. His *self nominated* opponent, S. A. Douglas, refuses to take issue with him upon the principles of that platform, but insists on arguing with him from radical resolutions passed at Aurora or Rockford *four* years ago, and *two* years before the Republican party of Illinois was formed! Or from Resolutions voted for by Anti-Nebraska members of the State Legislature of '54-5—eighteen months before the present Republican party had an existence. Why does Douglas dodge the Republican Bloomington State platform of '56? or the Springfield State platform of '58? or the National Philadelphia platform of 1856? Why resort to the highways and byways for a platform when the recognized, authoritative platforms of our party stand before him towering up like Egyptian pyramids? Because they are *unassailable*, and Lincoln standing on them, is also unassailable. Douglas dare not take issue with Lincoln on the recognized, expounded, and authoritative principles of the great Republican party, either State or national! That

is the reason he ducks and dodges, summersets and snivels.

———

MR. DOUGLAS' FIVE CHANGES ON THE SLAVERY QUESTION
October 8, 1858

Here the Editor seeks to undermine the effect of Douglas' arguments by establishing his unreliability. Lincoln subsequently acknowledged that without the support given him by THE TRIBUNE, *he would have been defeated overwhelmingly.*

That the people of Illinois look upon Mr. Douglas with distrust and accept his utterances with many grains of allowance need excite no wonder. They have learned from his teaching that whatever he may be to them, when on the stump, he is as constant as the needle to the pole in his devotion to the interests of the South, when in the Senate of the United States. Though repeatedly changing his front, he has never swerved from his allegiance to those from whom at last he hopes to receive the reward of his labor and the crowning glory of his ambition.

During Mr. Douglas' not very long Senatorial career, he has had five distinct lines of policy, with which he has abused, deceived and then betrayed the people who have made him all that he is. He was,

1st, A Democrat—this before his hopes of the Presidency were excited—in favor of the policy of Jefferson, which preserved all territory, not otherwise provided for, to Freedom.

5

2nd, An advocate of the Missouri Compromise, which, when the policy upon which that Compromise was based was acceptable to the South, he proposed to extend to the Pacific, and thus condemn the lower half of California and all of New Mexico to the curse of the "institution." Upon the demand of the South, he became,

3rd, The reputed father of the Kansas-Nebraska bill, which all over Illinois he defended upon the ground that the people of a Territory might, *through their Territorial Legislature,* admit or exclude slavery, as to them seemed best. Nine out of every ten of our readers have thus heard him maintain the people's right. He again changed his opinion, and became,

4th, A defender of the Dred Scott decision, which is an embodiment of John C. Calhoun's doctrine that slavery goes wherever the Constitution goes, and that there is no power either in the people or Congress to stay its progress. His speech at Springfield, before a political grand jury of the Supreme Court of the State, proves his identity here. Pressed by Lincoln, he has lately changed front again, and appears,

5th, As the reconciler of the contradiction between his previous ideas of popular sovereignty and the opposite opinions avowed by the highest judicial tribunal in the land. He seems to have aimed at the belief that a Territorial Legislature may set up a higher law for itself in opposition to that Federal tribunal, and by unfriendly police regulations, &c., &c., set at naught the Constitution of the country.

These are the five positions that Mr. Douglas has assumed; and every one of them he has defended as he now defends himself; and in behalf of every one he has made the same groundless and vulgar charges upon his opponents, that are the basis of his speeches in this campaign. We do not wonder then that the people turn a deaf ear to his pleadings and entreaties; that they have learned at last, that Mr. Douglas himself is the chief one of Mr. Douglas' cares, and that the gratification of his ambition by means of continued subservience to the South, is the end and aim of all his efforts in the dear people's behalf.

As these things become more clearly apparent, as his repeated changes—always for the worse— are exposed at the fire-side and the hustings, his audiences will continue to fall off; and before the canvass is over, we venture to predict, he will speak to his hired scribblers, his two gunners, and his powder-monkey, alone. Poor Little Dug!

———

MUTILATION OF LINCOLN'S SPEECH
October 11, 1858

THE TRIBUNE *and the* Democratic Press, *both then in financial difficulties, were consolidated in July, 1858. The paper was known as* THE PRESS AND TRIBUNE *until Oct. 25, 1860, when the present title was resumed.*

Among the varying versions of the Lincoln speeches, historians have accepted THE TRIBUNE'S *text as standard. It is the text which was used, with Lincoln's endorsement, when the de-*

bates where published in book form. The phonographic (i. e. shorthand) reporter who recorded the debates for THE TRIBUNE *was Robert R. Hitt.*

If mutilating public discourses were a criminal offence, the scamp whom Douglas hires to report Lincoln's speeches would be a ripe subject for the Penitentiary. The report of Mr. Lincoln's remarks at Galesburg are shamefully and outrageously garbled. Hardly a sentence he uttered has escaped defacement. Not a paragraph has been fairly reported, from the commencement to the conclusion of his speech. Some of his finest passages are disemboweled, and chattering nonsense substituted in their stead. Wherever Lincoln made a "hit," the sentence containing it is blurred, and the point carefully eviscerated. The fellow has even gone the length of suppressing the cheers and applause that so frequently greeted the remarks of Mr. Lincoln, while he has thickly interspersed Douglas' harangues with such ejaculations as "Great laughter," "Loud shouts," and "Tremendous cheers," when it is notorious that his remarks excited neither the one nor the other.

The editor of the *Times* puts on the finishing touch by running the sentences and paragraphs of Lincoln's speech together, regardless of sense or the rules of punctuation. Take for instance that part of his speech treating of the doctrine contained in the Dred Scott decision as applied to States. It is properly divisible into nine paragraphs, but the *Times* drives it into two. Look at the way it prints Mr. Lincoln's syllogism. And through all this portion of his speech, filling three fourths of a column, not one sentence of what he said is correctly reported in the *Times*. It is all garbled, emasculated, and defaced.

The reason for this dastardly and fraudulent conduct is plain enough. Douglas dare not allow his opponent to be correctly reported or correctly printed. He dare not let the full force of Lincoln's arguments go before his deluded followers. Hence, he and his organ resort to the base and cowardly trick of mutilating the language of his adversary uttered in debate. Douglas employs two phonographic puffers imported from abroad. He instructs them what to say and how to distort and pervert what his antagonist may say, and he pays them for these dishonorable services. His Chicago and St. Louis organs aid and abet him in this work of adulation of himself and detraction of his opponent.

Now contrast the course pursued by honest Abraham Lincoln. He keeps neither hired puffers nor paid libellers. He goes from one appointment to another without parade or ostentation. He charters no palatial cars with a bar-room and hotel aboard. He drags no cannon and powder monkeys after him to announce his coming or departure. He has never requested one of his speeches to be reported or published, nor has he seen or revised, before they appeared in type, any of his speeches in the five discussions that have taken place.

This paper employed an honest and accomplished phonographic reporter and directed him to make an accurate and impartial report of

7

each debate, and this has been faithfully done. Six times he has reported Mr. Douglas' speeches and as often the PRESS AND TRIBUNE has published them. No complaint has been entered or exceptions taken to the accuracy and fairness of these reports. Douglas himself admits that he has been correctly and excellently reported and printed in the PRESS AND TRIBUNE.

There are to be two more discussions, and we presume that on the part of Douglas and the *Times*, the same system of garbling and misprinting Lincoln's speeches, will be persisted in to the end of the chapter. The same scoundrelly means will be continued to break the force of Lincoln's blows, before they reach the Douglas worshippers. But these tricks will not avert the sure verdict of "guilty," which the jury of the people will render against the Demagogue on the third of November.

OUR LAST APPEAL
November 2, 1858

Every editorial writer knows the experience of coming to the last day of a political campaign in the certainty that the voters' minds are made up, beyond possibility of change. All that remains to be said on election morning is "Go and vote." The editorial which follows was included in the collection to show that when the editor understands what is at stake and feels it deeply enough, he can make this final admonition really count.

To the Polls!! To the Polls!!

CITIZENS OF CHICAGO:—This is the last appeal we can make to you in behalf of the Everlasting Right, before you cast your votes in the most important election you have ever participated in. For many months the eyes of the Union have been fastened upon you. From the forests of Maine to the lakes of Minnesota it is believed that the destiny of the American people hinges on the event in Illinois today. We believe so; you believe so. It is a most grave and serious trust which is reposed in your hands.

We presume you have settled clearly in your own minds which party upholds the principles that gave us birth as a nation—which stands by the Declaration of Independence in its high integrity— which declares the inalienable right of all men, in all lands, to life, liberty and the pursuit of happiness —which is striving to protect the Territories of the Union from the curse of human bondage. Then we have only to urge you to give the duty you owe to those principles, *today*. Trust in no result or majority until the last vote is in and the polls are closed.

We have every assurance that this first Republican city in the Union, will today roll up the largest majority she has ever given for Freedom. But to secure this every man must work. Go to the polls *early* and deposit your ballot. Then go among your friends and acquaintances and labor till the last vote which you can influence by fair means, is in the box where it belongs. Let no exigency of weather or business deter you. This election will never come again. If you make but one vote in a whole day's hard

8

work you will have deserved well of your country. LAY DOWN THIS PAPER. GO TO THE POLLS AND WORK.

A WORD TO CAMPAIGN SUBSCRIBERS
November 5, 1858

A legislative majority pledged to Douglas was elected, thanks largely to an apportionment that discriminated against the northern counties. The Republicans, however, carried their state ticket, 125,430 to 121,609.

This number of the PRESS AND TRIBUNE is the last that will be received by our Campaign Subscribers, without a renewal of their subscriptions. We are pained to say that they will read it with sorrow, because it conveys to them the sure intelligence of Mr. Lincoln's defeat—a result that we have labored zealously and earnestly to avoid.

We are beaten, but not disheartened or overawed. The principles and policy for which we have contended and shall still continue to contend, commend themselves with such convincing power to our judgment and conscience that we cannot be false to them if we would. That they are at no distant day to be triumphant in the parties of the country; that they are to control its legislation, and make it what our fathers intended it should be—the abiding place of Freedom and Justice —we have no doubt. To hasten that day, we shall continue to work.

Now friends, shall we have your aid? The time for effective action is now while the sting and mortification of defeat are felt. Now is the time for the renewal of honest vows to labor in behalf of Freedom's cause. Now is the time to put the elements of the next and the great campaign in motion. Now is the time to commence the instruction and enlightenment of the public mind in such a way that hereafter we shall mourn no such disasters as that by which we are overtaken. Shall we have your aid? We promise nothing, except to be true to our professions, and to leave nothing undone that will make the PRESS AND TRIBUNE worthy of your continued support. While paying such attention to political matters as the state of parties and the exigencies of the country demand, we shall by no means neglect what intimately concerns all into whose hands the paper will fall. The news of the day, correct commercial intelligence, and reliable information regarding the West and its varied interests, will each be afforded its appropriate space in our columns. We feel, nay, we know, that a paper published in the Northwest by Northwestern men wholly devoted to Northwestern interests, is far more valuable to our readers than one coming from another quarter of the Union where Western wants and Western tastes are neither consulted or understood.

Shall we continue to send you our paper? You have been a reader of it about four months. Whether it has displayed industry, tact and ability enough to commend it to your support, we leave you to decide. That its contents will be of more general and varied interest now that the excitement of the campaign is passed, you may be assured. That we shall be able to make it an ever-welcome visitor in your family—a source from which instruction, amusement and profit may be derived, we shall not fail to hope. To make it so good as to defy competition at home or abroad, will be our steady and constant aim. Will you go with us?

A WORD TO MESSRS. GREELEY & CO.

November 6, 1858

Here is early evidence of THE TRIBUNE'S *independence of seaboard leadership. The attitude has been persistent and will appear again in controversies over the tariff, monopolies, the rise of the Progressive party, Pittsburgh-plus, foreign policy, and numerous other matters.*

Medill had been the Cleveland correspondent of Greeley's New York TRIBUNE *and there is some evidence for the belief that Greeley suggested the move to Chicago. At the time, Greeley's influence in the west was very great, thanks to the wide circulation of his weekly edition. There never was any corporate connection between the two Tribunes; and their opinions, as in this instance, were frequently as divergent as their editors were always poles apart in character and temperament.*

We have no desire to make fresh sores, or irritate old ones, but we owe it to the Republican party—now shown to be the Republican *majority*—of Illinois, to exchange a word with certain people in the Eastern States who contributed to our practical defeat in the late con-

test. Let us come down to the "brass" of the thing at once. You, Messrs. Greeley & Co., argued to us in this way:

"Douglas is treacherous, as everybody knows. He has been pro-slavery all his life, but he will be anti-slavery in a moment if he can make anything by it. His quarrel with a few nigger drivers gives us a chance to make him an Anti-Slavery man. Re-elect him to the Senate and the job is done. Then we can beat old Buck and the Democracy in 1860." We defy you, gentlemen, to make any fairer statement of your case if you make a truthful one.

We replied as follows: "If we re-elect Mr. Douglas we surrender to him; we are in his power. Nobody pretends he is a Republican—he declares constantly he is not. He is a slaveholder. He has endorsed the Dred Scott decision in a way which not even his ingenuity can eradicate. He denies the first paragraph in the Declaration of Independence. He is steeped to his eyebrows in filibusterism and slavery propagandism. He has done nothing yet which the plantations will not forgive, with the explanation that his poverty, but not his will enabled him to oppose Lecompton. The Republican party in Illinois was not formed to elect pro-slavery Democrats to office. The argument upon which you base Mr. Douglas' claims to our support, viz: his political dishonesty—suffices us to let him take his own course, while we, ours. There is as great peril to Republicanism in 1860 in the trade you

OLD BUCK: President Buchanan.

10

propose, as in the square knockdown for which *we assume the responsibility.*"

These were our respective positions. In the element of honesty we take it there is no comparison to be instituted between them. We proposed to elect a Republican to the Senate. You proposed to elect a pro-slavery Democrat in the hope he would cheat other pro-slavery Democrats, instead of cheating you. So much for that. And on the score of sagacity the event has shown to our minds that the moral weight of the New York *Tribune* and those individuals who co-operate with it, thrown against us not only before our State Convention, but up to the day of election, has defeated us by a beggarly majority in the legislative districts. We judge that it is this mainly which has defeated us, and we judge from our personal knowledge of the influences which dragged our majority down in this city from 1200 to 800.

And so much for that. The same future now awaits all of us. We presume you have been actuated from the beginning by sincere hostility to slavery extension. Your way of accomplishing the end had in view was different from ours. We believe you committed an error of judgment. And that is all.

_____

ABRAHAM LINCOLN

November 10, 1858

Until Jan. 6, 1859, when the legislature met to elect a senator, many observers believed that President Buchanan would use what influence

he had among the Democratic members to deprive Douglas of the majority required for election. These expectations were not realized. Douglas was elected on the first ballot, receiving 54 votes to Lincoln's 41.

Mr. Lincoln is beaten. Though Presidential management and the treachery of pretended friends may prevent Mr. Douglas' return, Mr. Lincoln cannot succeed. We know of no better time than the present to congratulate him on the memorable and brilliant canvass that he has made. He has fully vindicated the partialities of his friends, and has richly earned, though he has not achieved, success.

He has created for himself a national reputation that is both envied and deserved; and though he should hereafter fill no official station, he has done in the cause of Truth and Justice, what will aways entitle him to the gratitude of his party and to the admiration of all who respect the high moral qualities and the keen, comprehensive, and sound intellectual gifts that he has displayed. No man could have done more. His speeches will become landmarks in our political history; and we are sure that when the public mind is more fully aroused to the importance of the themes which he has so admirably discussed, the popular verdict will place him a long way in advance of the more fortunate champion by whom he has been overthrown.

The Republicans owe him much for his truthfulness, his courage, his self-command, and his consistency; but the weight of their debt is chiefly in this: that, under no temptation, no apprehension of defeat, in com-

11

pliance with no solicitation, has he let down our standard in the least. That God-given and glorious principle which is the head and front of Republicanism, "All men are created equal, and are entitled to life, liberty and the pursuit of happiness," he has steadily upheld, defended, illustrated and applied in every speech which he has made. Men of his own faith may have differed with him when measures only were discussed; but the foundation of all—the principle which comprehends all—he has fought for with a zeal and courage that never flagged or quailed. In that was the pith and marrow of the contest.

Mr. Lincoln, at Springfield at peace with himself because he has been true to his convictions, enjoying the confidence and unfeigned respect of his peers, is more to be envied than Mr. Douglas in the Senate! Long live Honest Old Abe

———

THE FATAL FRIDAY

December 2, 1859

On the night of October 16, 1859, John Brown, the abolitionist, and his band of 18 seized the federal arsenal at Harper's Ferry, Va. Two days later they were overpowered. Ten of Brown's men and five on the other side were killed in the struggle. Brown's trial for treason, murder, and incitement of a slave rebellion opened on October 27 and was concluded on October 31.

Earlier editorials dealing with these incidents disclose anxiety lest Brown's act of violence cost the Republicans the support of moderates in the Presi-

dential election the following year. This editorial strikes a different, and prophetic note.

John Brown dies today! As Republicans, maintaining as we do, that neither individuals nor parties in the North have a right to interfere with slavery where it exists under the sanction of positive law in the States, we cannot say that he suffers unlawfully. The man's heroism which is as sublime as that of a martyr, his constancy to his convictions, his suffering, the disgraceful incidents of his trial, the poltroonry of those who will lead him forth to death, have excited throughout all the North strong feelings of sympathy in his behalf; but nowhere, within our knowledge, is the opinion entertained that he should not be held answerable for the consequence of his act.

As long as we are a part of the Union, consenting to the bond by which the States are bound together, supporting the constitution and the laws, and using the language and entertaining the sentiments of loyalty, we cannot join in the execration of the extreme penalty which the unfortunate and infatuated old man will suffer. We may question the wisdom of the method by which he is punished—may believe that Virginia would have added to her honor and confounded her enemies, by an act of clemency toward him and his associates—may condemn in unmeasured terms the cowardice and blood-thirstiness which her people have displayed—but when we question the right of a Sovereign State to inflict a penalty for so glaring and fatal an infraction of her

12

laws, we are advocating disunion in its most objectionable form. For that we are not prepared. We would be glad to avert the axe which hangs over the old man's head, if persuasion and entreaty would do it; but we see no way under Heaven by which, doing our duty as law-abiding citizens, we could counsel the use of force for his rescue, or by which we could join in a crusade against those by whom he has been legally though hastily, and because hastily, shamefully, condemned!

We are not debarred, however, the right of praising the inherent though mistaken nobleness of the man, of pitying the fanaticism which led him into his present strait, of regretting that a character which might have been so illustrious in the history of his country, must be loaded with the consequences of his errors.

To our more radical readers those views will be unpalatable; but they are such that Republicans must entertain. When the fanatical action of the South and the accumulated agressions with which she has affected the North, dissolve the ties that hold the North and South together, and when we no longer owe allegiance to the Constitution and laws which the propagandists of Slavery have long trodden under their feet, then we may have reason, upon the broadest principles of human right, to not only bless but aid any work that will assist in the emancipation, by arms if necessary, of every human being on American soil. Until that time comes there is but one course left. That we have pointed out.

We have firm belief that this execution of Brown will hasten the downfall of that accursed system against which he waged war. Throughout all this land, men will not fail to see that there is a conflict between the principles of humanity that have obtained a lodgment in every human heart, and obedience to laws which all have tacitly agreed to support. The shock caused by his death will be more than a nine days wonder. The emotions excited and the reflections provoked by the tragedy, will go to the very foundations of our political structure; and in all parts of the Union men will ask themselves how long this institution which compels men to put to death their fellows like Brown, who act upon motives and for objects that command the approbation of the world, shall be suffered to disgrace the age and the civilization in which we live. The question will reach hearts that have been callous heretofore; and ere many years it will bring the opposing forces which now distract the country—right on the one side and wrong on the other— enlightenment and barbarism— Christianity and Atheism—Freedom and Slavery—face to face for a final conflict.

We have no apprehension of the result, whenever it comes. The events of to-day bring it nearer than it has ever been before since the struggle began at Charlestown, Massachusetts, in 1775. It is ours, as it should have been Brown's, to labor and wait!

CHARLESTOWN (then in Virginia, now in West Virginia) was the scene of Brown's trial. This no doubt explains the reference in the concluding sentence to Charlestown, Mass. rather than the more familia: Lexington and Concord.

13

THE PRESIDENCY—
ABRAHAM LINCOLN

February 16, 1860

The Republican convention was to meet in Chicago in May to nominate a candidate for the Presidency. This editorial, setting forth the merits of Lincoln, is obviously directed to Republican leaders throughout the nation.

Of three or four States which are believed to constitute the debatable ground in the next Presidential campaign, and whose electoral votes will determine the result, Illinois is universally conceded to be one. It appears to be a foregone conclusion that the nomination of the Chicago Convention will be conferred upon no one who does not unite in himself the essential of requisite qualification, devotion to the distinctive principles of the Republican party, and availability in the States alluded to above.

We have no hesitation in saying that as respects the first two essentials, Abraham Lincoln, of Illinois, is the peer of any man yet named in connection with the Republican nominations, while in regard to availability, we believe him to be more certain to carry Illinois and Indiana than any one else, and his political antecedents are such as to commend him heartily to the support of Pennsylvania and New Jersey.

Mr. Lincoln would now be in the seat occupied by Mr. Douglas in the U. S. Senate, but for the gross unfairness of the apportionment of our legislative representation. In his contest with Mr. Douglas in 1858, less

AVAILABILITY: the ability to win.

than two hundred additional votes in close districts would have secured his triumph, bad as the apportionment was. At the same election the Republicans achieved a victory on their State officers—the vote of the latter being about equal to the aggregate vote of the Douglasites and Democrats. On the popular vote in the three Northern Congressional districts there was a Republican loss of several thousand growing out of the belief that Judge Douglas had permanently broken with the Democratic party, and the persistent manner in which Eastern Republicans and newspapers advocated his election. With Mr. Lincoln as our candidate for the Presidency, not only would all these votes be recovered, but greater or less inroads would be made in the ranks of the Democracy, and the State be secured beyond any possible contingency.

But the popularity of Mr. Lincoln is not confined to Illinois or to the Northwestern States. His memorable canvass with Mr. Douglas in 1858, gave Republicans throughout the Union an opportunity of becoming familiar with his admirable personal qualities, his entire devotion to the distinctive principles of the party, his rare abilities, and his broad, statesmanlike views of national political questions. We briefly sum up some of the elements of his popularity and strength:

1st. A gentleman of unimpeachable purity of private life. His good name is not soiled by a single act, political, social, moral or religious, that we or his friends need blush to own as his. In all his relations to his fellows he has not yet been guilty of

14

that thing upon which an enemy can place his finger and say, "this is dishonest," or "this is mean." Herein he is the peer of the most unspotted man in the Republic—the living likeness, full length size, of the best of the eminent characters who laid the foundation of the government.

2d. A man of, at once, great breadth and great acuteness of intellect. Not learned, in a bookish sense, but master of great fundamental principles, and of that kind of ability which applies them to crises and events. The masterly canvass which he made with Douglas, and his later speeches in Ohio, mark him as one of the ablest political thinkers of his day.

3d. Right on the record. An Old Line Whig of the Henry Clay school, originally, he came early into the Republican movement in which he has since been so conspicuous. He has that radicalism which a keen insight into the meaning of the anti-slavery conflict is sure to give; but, coupled with it, that constitutional conservatism which could never fail in proper respect for existing institutions and laws, and which would never precipitate or sanction innovations more destructive than the abuses that they seek to correct. Right on the question of Slavery, on the Homestead question, on all the issues which divide the parties; needing no tinkering to make him acceptable to Pennsylvania and New Jersey—candidate of the party which in itself is an embodiment of the principles and measures necessary for the perpetuity of the Union and the preservation of our free institutions—he would enter the field acceptable to the Opposition of all shades of opinion, harmonizing all interests, conciliating all jarring elements—the master of the position, a guarantor of success.

4th. A man of executive capacity. Never garrulous, never promising what he cannot perform, never doing anything for show or effect, laboriously attentive to detail, industrious and conscientious, he would see to it that no want of promptness, attention, or industry on his part should defeat the reforms in the administration of national affairs which Republicanism is pledged to inaugurate.

These are some of the reasons why we favor the nomination of Mr. Lincoln for the first place on the National Republican ticket. We do not know, however, that he has any aspirations for the position. While others are intriguing and trading, he is at his professional work, content to be let alone. But he is no doubt at the disposal of his friends; and we feel very confident that Illinois will present his name to the Chicago Convention, as the man, above all others, who will be most likely to lead the Republican party on to a glorious victory, and whose administration of the National Government would recall the best days of the Republic. Should the Convention give him this position, then the honor which he has not sought, but which his admirers have hoped he might attain, will, like ripe fruit, fall into his hands. Abraham Lincoln will never be President by virtue of intrigue and bargain.

15

A LAST ENTREATY

May 18, 1860

The convention met on May 16 and the climax was reached on the day this forceful exposition of Lincoln's political strengths and Seward's weaknesses was published. The editorial is the more effective for the fact that neither candidate is mentioned by name.

The presumption that the Republicans are to succeed by reason of the division of their opponents, rather than by their own inherent strength and the cohesive power of their principles; and that a man objectionable, on the ground of a want of availability, to the six doubtful States, Connecticut, Rhode Island, New Jersey, Pennsylvania, Indiana and Illinois, must be nominated at all hazards—is too dangerous to obtain currency among shrewd and sagacious men.

That with a victory within our grasp, if that prudence is exercised which the crisis demands, there should be any number of delegates, who, for the sake of promoting the fortunes and gratifying the ambition of any living man, dare to stake all upon the contingency of a Democratic disruption, rather than throw themselves back upon the certain and reliable strength of the party opposed to the extension of Human Slavery, is too monstrous for belief. And that these delegates cannot see that the nomination most strenuously insisted upon by a large minority is that which, more than all other causes combined, would compel the settlement of the disputes and dissensions in the Democratic ranks,

and force us to make head against an united and unscrupulous party, is incomprehensible. Not that alone —that they do not also see that we must make the fight, in that contingency, without the aid of a large share of the 175,000 votes in those six States cast for Mr. Fillmore in 1856, and now claimed for John Bell and Edward Everett, is the most fatal feature of this otherwise plain matter.

It is natural that gentlemen from the strong Republican States of Vermont, New York, Michigan, Wisconsin and Minnesota, where the action of the party is with difficulty kept within the safe and wholesome limitations of the Philadelphia Platform, should look with distrust upon any representations which set forth the actual condition of political affairs in the six states that we have named, and the difficulties which the nomination of a certain candidate will throw in the way of success. We can conceive that they— coming from localities in which Republicanism has deep and firm root, cannot understand why it is that Illinois, Indiana and Pennsylvania, populated in part by emigrants or the descendants of emigrants from the Slave States, should have the fears by which they are tormented; and why it is that, without exception, all their leading men in private station, their candidates in nomination for State offices, their most farsighted politicians, and their most ardent friends of the Republican cause, should declare that the policy which a few of the States that are certain for any Republican candidate, and a few others that cannot give any appreciable support to the

16

ticket under any circumstances whatever, seem determined to pursue, is, if not the precursor of defeat, at least the opening of a fearful struggle, the end of which is involved in great obscurity and doubt.

But let us point them to a matter of history—a permanent evidence of the opinion of Indiana and Illinois —which will, to all fair minds, carry correct knowledge of public opinion in those States. We refer to the Black laws—statutes than which none are more infamously despotic and unjust in Naples or Grand Cairo —which the Republican party in neither State has ever been able to repeal. By these, Slavery is virtually established within the jurisdiction of the two States, and any horseblock in either may any day be made the auction stand at which men are bought and sold. Here is a fact—not an opinion of some half mad zealot—which none can gainsay; glaring public evidence in the statute book of the true condition, the average enlightenment of the popular mind on this negro question in Indiana and Illinois.

We ask, we entreat, we implore, that a candidate inside of the Republican party, radical up to the extreme limit of the platform but not obnoxious to the charges which will be urged by the so-called De-

THE BLACK LAWS: By a statute adopted in 1853, Illinois imposed a heavy fine on any Negro, bond or free, who entered the state. If the fine was not paid, the Negro was to be sold at public auction to the person bidding the shortest period of service for the payment of the fine. The anti-slavery forces in the legislature were heavily outnumbered and the best they could do was to win approval of a provision requiring jury trial.

mocracy against one prominent gentleman now in the field and in high favor, may be selected, to the end that a triumph may not be a thing of infinite labor, and prolonged and painful doubt, but a certainty from the moment that the choice of the Convention is declared. Let us, speaking in behalf of a larger circle of Republican readers than can be claimed by any other journal west of New York, let us, who have labored so long and, we hope, so acceptably, for the Republican cause, warn the Convention that the voice of the united doubtful States cannot, must not be disregarded.

They are six, if not seven, in number. They are as ardently devoted to the general principles of the party as any others. They recognize the necessity for success, that the good name of the country, imperilled by the disgraceful Administration now in power, may be restored; that the Union, now threatened by the Democracy, may be preserved; that the Republican organization, upon which the hopes of the country now hang, may be kept from the dissolution which a defeat foreshadows. They cast seventy-five electoral votes. They are potent, and their approbation of the nominee, not only here at Chicago, but at the polls in November, must be secured, else an inglorious and fatal defeat stares us in the face. For the sake of all that the party would accomplish, we entreat the Convention to act with the prudence, wisdom and foresight which the crisis demands. We believe that all will yet be well.

17

LINCOLN AS HE IS

May 23, 1860

A profile of Lincoln, drawn by a devoted friend. The editorial was widely copied by newspapers in the north, as was undoubtedly the intention. It was included also in the campaign biography written by John L. Scripps.

Ten thousand inquiries will be made as to the looks, the habits, tastes and other characteristics of Honest Old Abe. We anticipate a few of them.

Mr. Lincoln stands six feet and four inches high in his stockings. His frame is not muscular, but gaunt and wiry; his arms are long, but not unreasonably so for a person of his height; his lower limbs are not disproportioned to his body. In walking, his gait though firm is never brisk. He steps slowly and deliberately, almost always with his head inclined forward and his hands clasped behind his back.

In matters of dress he is by no means precise. Always clean, he is never fashionable; he is careless but not slovenly. In manner he is remarkably cordial, and, at the same time, simple. His politeness is always sincere but never elaborate and oppressive. A warm shake of the hand and a warmer smile of recognition are his methods of greeting his friends.

At rest, his features though those of a man of mark, are not such as belong to a handsome man; but when his fine dark gray eyes are lighted up by any emotion, and his features begin their play, he would be chosen from among a crowd as one who had in him not only the kindly sentiments which women love, but the heavier metal of which full grown men and Presidents are made. His hair is black, and though thin is wiry. His head sits well on his shoulders, but beyond that it defies description. It nearer resembles that of Clay than that of Webster; but is unlike either. It is very large and, phrenologically, well proportioned, betokening power in all its developments. A slightly Roman nose, a widecut mouth and a dark complexion, with the appearance of having been weather-beaten, completes the description.

In his personal habits, Mr. Lincoln is as simple as a child. He loves a good dinner and eats with the appetite which goes with a great brain; but his food is plain and nutritious. He never drinks intoxicating liquors of any sort, not even a glass of wine. He is not addicted to tobacco, in any of its shapes. He never was accused of a licentious act in all his life. He never uses profane language. A friend says that once, when in a towering rage in consequence of the efforts of certain parties to perpetrate a fraud on the State, he was heard to say "They shan't do it, d-n'em!" but beyond an expression of that kind, his bitterest feelings never carry him. He never gambles; we doubt if he ever indulges in any games of chance.

He is particularly cautious about incurring pecuniary obligations for any purpose whatever, and in debt, he is never content until the score is discharged. We presume he owes no man a dollar. He never speculates. The rage for the sudden acquisition of wealth never took hold of him. His gains from his profession have been moderate, but sufficient for his purposes. While others have dreamed of gold, he has been in pursuit of knowledge. In all his dealings he has the reputation of being generous but exact, and, above all, religiously honest. He would be a bold man who would say that Abraham Lincoln ever wronged any one out of a cent, or ever spent a dollar that he had not honestly earned. His struggles in early life have made him careful of money; but his generosity with his own is proverbial.

He is a regular attendant upon religious worship, and though not a communicant, is a pew-holder and liberal supporter of the Presbyterian Church, in Springfield, to which Mrs. Lincoln belongs. He is a scrupulous teller of the truth—too exact in his notions to suit the atmosphere of Washington as it now is. His enemies may say that he tells Black Republican lies; but no man ever charged that, in a professional capacity, or as a citizen dealing with his neighbors, he would depart from the Scriptural command.

At home he lives like a gentleman of modest means and simple tastes. A good sized house of wood, simply but tastefully furnished; surrounded by trees and flowers, is his own, and there he lives, at peace with himself, the idol of his family, and for his honesty, ability and patriotism, the admiration of his countrymen.

If Mr. Lincoln is elected President, he will carry but little that is ornamental to the White House. The country must accept his sincerity, his ability and his honesty, in the mould in which they are cast. He will not be able to make as polite a bow as Frank Pierce, but he will not commence anew the agitation of the Slavery question by recommending to Congress any Kansas-Nebraska bills. He may not preside at the Presidential dinners with the ease and grace which distinguish the "venerable public functionary," Mr. Buchanan; but he will not create the necessity for a Covode Committee and the disgraceful revelations of Cornelius Wendell. He will take to the Presidential chair just the qualities which the country now demands to save it from impending destruction—ability that no man can question, firmness that nothing can overbear, honesty that never has been impeached, and patriotism that never despairs.

JOHN COVODE, a Republican congressman, was chairman of a house committee which investigated charges that money and patronage had been used by President Buchanan to influence congressmen.

CORNELIUS WENDELL, Congressional printer, had testified before a senate committee to the payment of large sums exacted from him by Democratic politicians.

————

THE REAL ISSUE

January 3, 1861

South Carolina had adopted its ordinance of secession on Dec. 20, 1860, two weeks before this editorial appeared. Mississippi was to follow on Jan. 9, 1861, Florida on the 10th, and Alabama on the 11th. By Jan. 26 they had been joined by Georgia and Louisiana.

What a sight! The leading politicians of a great and once liberty-loving and patriotic party, the chief executive officers of the government, a full half of the people of one section of the Republic, all plotting and conspiring against the perpetuity of the fairest political fabric ever built by human hands, and provoking civil war between brothers—for what? That the representatives of a little Oligarchy of 347,000 slave-holders may have the privilege, not authorized by the Constitution, of buying, selling, working without pay and whipping at will, men, women and children in the Territories which God made free; that the Constitution which was purposely framed so that the word "slave" might not occur therein, may be so amended, after seventy years successful working, as to recognize property in man; that the States which have rid themselves of the crime and curse of involuntary bondage shall be compelled to accept it again; and that the moral sense of the people of the North, now rebelling against manselling, shall correct itself, and begin to affirm that the Atheism which makes one man own another is the new evangel for the civilization of mankind.

What a sight! What a theme for the historian who writes the Rise and Fall of the Republic of the United States! What a commentary on the civilization of the age! What a burning reproach to the cause of Democracy throughout the world! Yet we state fairly the causes of the quarrel. No difference of race and lineage, of religious faith, nor save in one thing, of political policy, has brought on the struggle. We are one people, with one hope and men have believed, with one destiny. That People is to be divided, that hope given up, and that glorious destiny

overruled, that the business of man-stealing and woman-whipping may grow with our nation's growth.

It is well enough in times like these, to keep the real issues steadily before the people. We state them above in language that all may understand.

A MODEST QUERY
February 16, 1861

Feb. 4-8, 1861. Delegates of the six seceding states, meeting at Montgomery, Ala., framed and adopted a provisional constitution.

Feb. 9. Jefferson Davis of Mississippi elected president of the Confederacy; Alexander H. Stephens of Georgia, vice-president.

Feb. 18. Jefferson Davis inaugurated.

In the months between the election and the inauguration of Lincoln, many so-called compromises were proposed. The Editor here raises an indignant voice against a surrender of principle, of the sort that three-quarters of a century later came to be called appeasement.

THE CHICAGO TRIBUNE has generally been accounted a Republican journal of conservative proclivities. It did some service in the good cause anterior to the nomination of Lincoln and continued its labors until he was elected. It has been usually recognized as an earnest, out-spoken and a reliable monitor and guide.

Suppose when the last contest was at its heighth—say a month before election, when the threats of disunion and revolution were as thick and just as alarming as they are to-day—THE TRIBUNE had astonished its readers—among others certain pork men and Water street grocers—

by an unconditional abandonment of the Platform of the party, and an adhesion to the Danite or Breckinridge plan for regulating the status of all the territory in the United States that will ever be threatened with the encroachments of Slavery —what would have been said? What term would have been severe enough, what denunciations bitter enough to express the mortification and rage of its Republican readers? The names of its editors and proprietors would have been synonyms of treachery and rascality; and they would barely have escaped personal violence at the hands of those whom they had betrayed.

We ask—Is not the truth in October, the truth in February? We ask again—As men who are shaping and moulding the opinions of the people of the Northwest, as we devoutly believe for a patriotic purpose, what would be thought of us, if any loafer could shake his fist under our editorial noses and coerce us into a disavowal of the sentiments which we entertain and which this journal proclaims? We need not answer the question—our readers will do that.

Apply the foregoing to the state of facts now existing and see where the shame is. Is not slavery the same monster of hideous mien that we contended against with such special earnestness from May to November? Is its extension into the national domain, under constitutional guaranties, any less a great crime now

DANITE: An anti-Douglas Democrat in 1858.

than then? No man can say No! to these questions.

Why then shall we be blamed if we continue on that road in which all Republicans agreed to travel? Why, if we ought not to submit to threats at home, and write under the impulse of personal fear,—shall we quail when a State threatens? Have the issues changed? No. Has Right lapsed into Wrong? No. Why then give way? Because, say the submissionists, there's the South in a threatening attitude, and if you and those like you persevere in the way in which conscience and patriotism point, she will do some desperate thing; perhaps she will secede, trade will be injured, and you as well as we shall suffer loss— in other words, there's that threatening ruffian with his fist under your nose—now surrender!

No, gentlemen, no! Truth is not a chameleon. Principle ante-dates policy. Duty outweighs interest. Love of Liberty is stronger than love of pelf, are maxims upon which THE TRIBUNE is conducted. If Republicans do not like its course, let them drop it. It may err, misjudge, be hasty, passionate, possibly intolerant, at times; but they shall never have reason to say that it was false to its principles or that it quailed before threats. For very shame, it could not if it would, be to-day what it was not yesterday—this year what it was not last year. Let others cringe and go their way. We stand to the colors.

21

EVERY MAN'S DUTY

April 16, 1861

April 12, 1861: Ft. Sumter attacked.
April 14: Ft. Sumter evacuated.
April 15: Lincoln summons 75,000 militiamen into federal service.

Lenity and forbearance have only nursed the viper into life—the war has begun! It may not be the present duty of each one of us to enlist and march to the sound of bugle and drum; but there is a duty, not less important, which is in the power of every man and woman in Chicago, and in the North, to perform—it is to be loyal in heart and word to the cause of the United States. From this hour, let no Northern man or woman tolerate in his or her presence the utterance of one word of treason. Let expressed rebuke and contempt rest on every man weak enough to be anywhere else in this crisis than on the side of the country against treason—of Lincoln and Scott against Davis and Twiggs—of God against Baal. We say to the Tories and lickspittles in this community, a patient and reluctant, but at last an outraged and maddened people, will no longer endure your hissing. You must keep your venom sealed, or go down! There is a Republic! The gates of Janus are open; the storm is on us. Let the cry be, THE SWORD OF THE LORD AND OF GIDEON!

MAJ. GEN. DAVID EMANUEL TWIGGS, (1790-1862), a Georgian, was in command of United States forces in Texas when, in February, 1861, he surrendered his men and stores to the Confederacy. He was dishonorably discharged from the United States army and shortly afterward was commissioned a major general in the Confederate army.

THE DUTY OF NEWSPAPERS

October 3, 1861

The classic statement of the role of the newspaper in time of war.
The war had been going badly and THE TRIBUNE *had been under severe criticism for saying so and naming names. The occasion for the editorial was the disclosure in* THE TRIBUNE *of incompetence and worse at the headquarters of Gen. Fremont in St. Louis. He is the "popular idol" referred to.* THE TRIBUNE *had supported him for the Presidency in 1856, had hailed his appointment to the western command, and had endorsed his attempts to emancipate the slaves in Missouri. The duty of exposing his derelictions was a painful one, but it was not shirked.*

The country is engaged in a war upon which hang momentous consequences, not alone to our government considered as an impersonation of the nation's dignity and honor but to every man, woman, and child living beneath our country's flag. It is a war for national existence, and for individual freedom, and prosperity, and happiness. It comes home to every man's hearth; it touches him nearly in all the relations of life, is a part of his daily thoughts and his secret prayers. For the time it is the universal business.

Our interest in it is not less than our neighbor's. Our feelings are as vitally concerned, our property is as seriously imperiled by want of success now, or complete failure by and by. But we cannot regard it alone from an individual and selfish standpoint. We have duties to the public which we must discharge.

By their own assumptions, or by quasi-popular consent, leading and influential journals like our own are in some sort regarded as watchmen on the walls, to look for approach of danger toward what their readers hold dear. They have had thrust upon them the duty, not always pleasant, of acting as conservators of the public good, often at the expense of their private interests. Men look to them not only for facts but for opinions. They do not often create, but they shape and give direction to public sentiment. They are the narrators of facts, the exponents of policy, the enemies of wrong.

Their office, in time of war, is not a whit less responsible, though infinitely more delicate, than in a period of peace. They deal with excited opinion, with passions painfully aroused, and with fears that know no reason. Their duties are quadrupled and their liabilities to the public indefinitely magnified. On that account they should not shrink from the responsibilities of their position. As dangers thicken, their courage should rise to meet them. To avoid expression of what high public interests demand, because of probable offense to this class or that or because of prospective loss of peace, would be to cowardly abandon duty and float with the current for safety.

We need not say that THE TRIBUNE, whatever its other faults, has not that of timidity. We are not of those who believe that, because the country is in danger and all private interests are threatened, or because military power overrides the civil law, it is the province of journalism of the better sort to keep silence when incompetency undertakes the management of public affairs, or hold its peace when unblushing rascality under the guise of patriotism is doing its deadly work.

We know of no reason that exempts the military man from criticism and, if necessary, vigorous denunciation, that does not apply to the civil servant in public life. There is nothing specially sacred in epaulets though worn by a popular idol. On the contrary, we hold it to be a duty to denounce all who stand in the way of the triumph of the good cause, and it matters little to us whether those who impede it are of our own faith and party or belong avowedly to the enemy. The safety and the honor of the country are at stake, and the peril is greater to-day from certain of our friends than from Beauregard and Davis.

It would be as recreant and cowardly not to speak out plainly as on the field of battle to refuse to fire at the foe. The country, we say, is in danger. Its salvation is the first duty of every man who loves it. Parties, private interests, personal safety are nothing when they stand in the way of the one grand object to be accomplished. We know our duty in the emergency and intend honestly and fearlessly to do it.

We know what the peril is which attaches to plain talking. We know that our personal interests would be better served oftentimes by silence than by honest speech. We know that thrift follows fawning. But, at the same time, we know how wholly and devotedly we love this republic and its institutions, and how ready

23

we are to do anything or brave anything so that we can most effectually serve them.

We make no claim to infallibility. Error is as common to us as to others, but in what we say and do, in this woeful crisis, we profess to be animated by motives as unselfish and by patriotism as pure as belong to men anywhere.

We bid our contemporaries, then, who would rather be victorious over THE TRIBUNE than over Jeff Davis, howl on. We have had the whole of them on our track in times before now and know just the sound of their bark and the danger from their bite. We go our own way, at our own time, in our own manner, in company of our own choosing, knowing as we do that vindication will be sure to follow. We can afford to be honest, and fearless, and to wait.

————

TOWARD EMANCIPATION

October 11, 1861

Emancipation presented a difficult constitutional problem as well as a problem of conscience to Lincoln. He hated slavery but had pledged himself repeatedly not to interfere with it in the states where its existence was lawful. In the end, he solved the dilemma by asserting that the Constitution conferred extraordinary powers on the Executive in time of war, precisely as suggested in the paragraphs which follow. They were published almost a year before the decision was taken. Here we present only the concluding lines of a much longer editorial, entitled "The Demands of Loyalty."

It is not even necessary that men should believe that slavery is an evil, in order to enlist them against it. For the argument's sake, we will call it a blessing—a humane, beneficent, Christian institution. What then? This excellent institution has grown strong. It is becoming more powerful than our Government, and threatens to engulf and swallow it up. Good as it may be, or as we may fancy it to be, it has inaugurated a civil war; and if unrestrained is certain to terminate our national existence. Then as loyal men we must sacrifice it. "If thy right eye offend thee, pluck it out and cast it from thee."

In any view that we may take, we arrive at the same conclusion, and that is, that loyalty and patriotism demand an unanimous public opinion in favor of such military action as will insure the most speedy overthrow of this wicked rebellion, and that action is embraced in one word —*emancipation*—if not emancipation by act of Congress or the proclamation of the President, emancipation as a military necessity. If not the emancipation of all slaves, those at least of rebel masters, remembering all the while that loyal slaveholders who observe the obligations of the Constitution have claims that other loyal men cannot afford to disregard.

————

THE CHICAGO TRIBUNE

July 23, 1862

"Our general fault is to be in advance of public opinion."

We can afford, at this time, when the direction of the popular opinion

24

of the country and the army is indubitably tending toward that goal at which THE TRIBUNE long ago arrived, to congratulate our thirty thousand daily subscribers in the Northwest—the men who through good and evil report have adhered to us—some because they loved plain and honest speaking, some because they agreed with us from the beginning, and some because they were curious to know what THE TRIBUNE had to say,—we can afford to congratulate them on the great change which has been wrought in this portion of the Union, since we commenced our labors for a more vigorous and comprehensive policy in the conduct of the war.

The change is indeed wonderful, and no less wonderful than timely and necessary. When we began to throw bombshells at do-nothing, pro-slavery generals, and stupid orders like Order No. 3; when we began to denounce the tomfoolery which would not permit black men to do their share in the terrific struggle, and which sent them back to their masters to work for the rebels; when we became the advocates of emancipation—compensated emancipation in the Border States—emancipation at the point of the bayonet in all States that had committed treason against the Fed-

eral Government; when in every issue we urged upon the Administration the employment of all the means permitted by our advanced civilization, more vigor, more severity, more activity and more zeal, —we were threatened as no newspaper guiltless of purposely outraging public sensibility, was ever threatened before. Not a day passed in which anonymous letters from cowardly assailants, and real warnings from timid friends did not command and adjure us to desist, and save ourselves from ruin and our printing establishment from destruction.

And more than once, and among men who should have known better, the plan of getting up a riot which should silence us, has been attempted; and more than one cowardly rascal offered to lead it if he could get a hundred men to back him. A simultaneous attack in country and city, by politicians, rival newspapers, and semi-secessionists, was made upon our circulation, to cut it down to a figure lower than that of the aggregate circulation of all the other daily papers in Chicago. And as one of the proprietors of THE TRIBUNE happened, by Mr. Lincoln's favor, to be Postmaster, a rush was made to upset him and put some less earnest and less patriotic man in his place. In a word, malevolence, indulged within the limits of reasonable discretion, ex-

ORDER NO. 3 was issued by Gen. Halleck on Nov. 20, 1861 after he had succeeded Gen. Fremont in the Missouri command. The order forbade fugitive slaves to enter the Union lines and required the army to expel any slaves who had been given refuge. Fremont's experiment in emancipation had delighted anti-slavery men but aroused the indignation of the conservatives, particularly in the border states. Order No. 3 produced precisely the opposite effect. Halleck was soon obliged to issue an interpretation of his directive that, for all practical purposes, nullified it.

JOHN LOCKE SCRIPPS (1818-66), one of the proprietors of THE TRIBUNE, was appointed postmaster of Chicago in 1861 and served for four years. He was the author of the first biography of Lincoln, a 32-page booklet published as a campaign tract in 1860 by THE CHICAGO TRIBUNE and also by the New York Tribune. Scripps wrote the book in Springfield with Lincoln's assistance.

hausted itself to do us injury, and make our influence in the West less potent than it has proved.

Lo, what a change! The whole country is at this moment almost abreast of THE TRIBUNE; and the doctrines and policy upon which it insisted, against such opposition, and with such a thorough and enlightened conviction of their necessity, are now commending themselves with overwhelming force to the favor of the whole people; and men who hardly sixty days ago, delighted to abuse their self-respect by saying that they were "conservatives," opposed to all "rash measures," to reducing this to a "nigger war," to "allowing black men to fight," are now ready to make affidavit that they were all wrong, and that the well abused and everywhere read CHICAGO TRIBUNE had, of all the journals in the country, the clearest insight into the nature, duration and cost of the struggle, and the best idea of the policy by which that struggle could be terminated for the glory of the Republic.

This is a compliment to our far-sightedness, to the correctness of our judgments of men, and to our intimate knowledge of the wide field of operations, that would make less modest men strut themselves out of their journalistic breeches. But we claim only the honor of having been right, when error was the rule; the credit of having looked deep into the causes and character of the contest, when limited views and feeble comprehension were the baneful fashion; and the praise which should always be awarded those, who, from a sense of duty, dare brave an excited

and angry public opinion. That is our claim; and the voice of the Northwest will award us all we ask.

We take this occasion to warn those who have been honestly influenced by the clamor that has been raised, that our general fault is to be in advance of public sentiment. We have means of obtaining intelligence, from which the public is debarred. We have quick instincts, and are not slow in forming accurate judgments of men and things. We have studied the whole question in the light of history and philosophy. Hence it is not wonderful that we should be in advance. We shall be so again. Some fine morning we shall pain our friends and gratify our enemies by an article challenging their criticism, and shocking their pre-conceived opinions; and another contest and another period of attempted persecution will only bring us out as now, ahead with banners flying, proving again that in what makes a powerful if not popular journal, THE TRIBUNE will remain unsurpassed—the great newspaper and leading organ of opinion in the West.

____

SUPPORT THE GOVERNMENT

September 24, 1862

On Sept. 22, 1862, Lincoln announced that 100 days later, on Jan. 1, 1863, he would issue a proclamation emancipating the slaves in states still in rebellion.

During all the time that we have labored for the overthrow of slavery in the revolted States, as at once the

26

cause and support of the rebellion, we have been charged by the opposite party with "opposing the government." The charge was untrue, and known to be so by those who made it, for our columns have borne daily testimony for eighteen months to our zeal in forwarding every measure, in field or council, for the most vigorous prosecution of the war, for the largest armies, for the heaviest taxes—in a word, for "the most stupendous preparations" for crushing armed traitors that Stephen A. Douglas counselled with his latest breath.

All this we have done with an eye single to the glory of the Union, and the perpetuity of its free institutions. We have not hesitated to urge what we deemed the proper policy to be pursued in regard to slavery, but when we have found that our ideas were not adopted by those to whom the destinies of the nation were lawfully entrusted, we have not abated a jot or tittle of our unfaltering support of the government in *all* its efforts to crush the rebellion, and preserve the priceless treasures committed to its hands.

Now we ask of those, who have heretofore chided us in no measured terms, *that they too shall support the Government.* We intend to give it the same unconditional aid and encouragement that it has always received at our hands, and we shall hope to make it the more effective, as we believe that liberty is the life giving spirit of the Union, and slavery its deadly poison. Is it unreasonable that we ask those who have differed from us, as patriots and lovers of their country, to give

the government their support, now that emancipation is to be proclaimed as the last weapon wherewith to strike down the rebellion?

We speak only to true men and patriots. To those who love slavery better than their country and their country's flag, and who echo the atrocious sentiment of the Chicago *Times*, that "the Government, by the act of the President, is itself in rebellion," we have only to say that the sooner they shoulder muskets and step into the ranks of Jeff. Davis, the sooner will they take their true places and act out the real sentiment of their hearts. But the great body of the people, Democrats as well as Republicans, will come up as one man to the support of the government in its faithful efforts to preserve the Union. Upon the heaven defying traitors who have drawn the sword against their country rests the responsibility of the act. They can even now prevent its taking effect by laying down their arms and returning to their allegiance. If *they* choose that the blow shall fall let it fall, and let all the people say Amen!

———

OUR COUNTRY'S FUTURE

September 28, 1864

The 19th century's faith in man's moral as well as his material progress is well exemplified in this editorial forecasting the trend of national development after the war. The text here is slightly abridged.

The spectacle of our reunited country, resuming its onward march to material prosperity and empire, after

27

the interruption caused by the war, with the Union maintained, the Government disenthralled and regenerated, and Slavery, the sole cause of dissension, obliterated, dedicating our whole land to freedom and our whole people to enlightenment, civilization and Christianity, without a stain on our flag, or a foe to our unity, is one well calculated to fill our hearts with hope, and to reconcile us to the fierce ordeal through which we are passing.

In the regenerated Union the poor man will everywhere feel that his toil is honorable and his position as a citizen as respectable as that of the capitalist. In the restored Union the free school, a free press, and free speech will be enjoyed by all without asking leave of some adjacent owner of a thousand slaves. The poor man may hear the gospel preached without its being strained through the sieve of some committee of manstealers until the text "love they neighbor as thyself" shall read "buy thy neighbor for thyself." Skilled labor shall result from general education and not only shall schools, colleges and churches take the place of exhausted tobacco fields, immense rice swamps and pine barrens, but railroads shall spring up in fugitive paths, the bay of the bloodhound shall give place to the hum of the manufactory, the bleeding slave to the patent reaper, and the bowie knife and the bludgeon shall disappear before the principle of the equal brotherhood of man by right of the universal fatherhood of God. Southern barbarism, the concomitant of slavery, and brought with it by necessity from Dahomey and Congo, shall yield to Northern freedom, equality and enlightenment, the fruit of centuries of European growth and development, ripened and perfected in our noonday of American freedom.

When our land shall thus have been made one, and our people redeemed through the atonement of blood, in which the God of nations has from all time decreed that national sins shall be blotted out and national virtues born anew, what shall prevent the American Union from being, thenceforth the crowning national work of the Almighty, the wonder of the world? Shall Slavery forbid? It will not exist. Shall Abolitionism? It will be swallowed up in liberty. Shall sectional pride? Each section will have that only of which all sections will be proud—labor dignified—wealth and intelligence diffused and all the objects of our Union confirmed to all its people.

Europe will open her gates like a conquered city. Her people will come forth to us subdued by admiration of our glory and envy of our perfect peace. On to the Rocky Mountains and still over to the Pacific our mighty populations will spread, like the stars of heaven throughout the canopy of night, but like them controlled by the power of a great attraction operating on a unity of nature. Our thirty millions will be tripled in thirty years. Our thirty-four states will become an hundred. The planets do not glide more silently around the central sun than these will obey with a harmony like the "music of the spheres" —the central Government.

Cities will spring up everywhere as by magic; our trade, manufactures and commerce will rule the world; our light will fill—our liberty will pervade it. Coleridge's august conception of "the possible destiny of the United States of America as a nation of a hundred millions of freemen, stretching from the Atlantic to the Pacific, living under the laws of Alfred and speaking the language of Shakespeare and Milton," will be surpassed by the far more august realization.

For a hundred years to come historians will be engaged in placing in their true light the events which are now transpiring. What wonder that many of the present day do not rightly comprehend a march of events which will form a study for future ages—as have the periods of Themistocles, Caesar, Cromwell and Napoleon, for those which followed them? For a century to come military skill will consist in a knowledge of the changes in military science now being wrought; Republican statesmanship will consist in a thorough acquaintance with the principles of government now being contended for and settled in battle. The fame of orators will be founded upon their ability to portray in glowing terms of eulogy the heroism of our people and to connect their success with the principles of truth, and liberty. The reputations of artists will be made by immortalizing on canvas the fields of Donelson, Vicksburg and Mission Ridge, and the still more imposing scene yet to be witnessed of the capture of Charleston and the surrender of Richmond. But of one fact we may rest

assured. While the present age looks at it mainly as a struggle for Union and nationality, the future will regard as equally important what we regard as but an incident, viz: the regeneration of the Republic and the vindication of true democracy and of the rights of labor, by the abolition of slavery.

Not willingly, even for a future or a fame so glorious, would the people of the free North have entered upon the present contest. But we may still look through the stormy present into the near and bright future, borrowing of the provision which there awaits us. These hopes sustain us. We are living in times that try men's souls. Half a century hence to have lived in this age will be fame. To have served it well will be immortality. Think of this, and when you cast your vote in November, vote for the unity of the republic, for the rights of man and for the only candidates who represent them—Abraham Lincoln, of Illinois and Andrew Johnson, of Tennessee.

———

THE GREAT CALAMITY

April 17, 1865

This editorial is selected from among a number dealing with the assassination.

Lincoln was shot on the evening of April 14 and died on the morning of the 15th. His program for the political and economic reconstruction of the south died with him.

The most horrid crime ever committed on this globe since wicked Jews crucified the Savior of mankind was perpetrated by rebel emissaries, in the assassination of the great, wise, and good Abraham Lincoln, and by a strange coincidence the murder was committed on the anniversary of Christ's death. On Good Friday the Savior expiated the sins of the world by a death on the cross, and the same day the greatest and best of living men was assassinated.

The foolish rebels have killed their best friend. The man who stood between them and retribution, who alone had the will and power to shield them from the punishment their crimes deserve, is slain by them. President Lincoln has mourned over the rebellious conduct of the insurgents as a father mourns over the conduct of an erring child. His heart bled for them. He sought to allure them back to the path of loyalty by excessive kindness and parental forgiveness. He never touched the hair on one of their guilty heads, but with sorrow and reluctance. He was preparing for them the feast of the Prodigal son. He was ready to welcome them back, and kill the fatted calf for their entertainment.

No man but Abraham Lincoln could restrain the American people from visiting righteous wrath upon the heads of the wicked leaders of the accursed rebellion. No living man possessed the confidence and affection of the people and army as he. To the judgment of no other man would they defer so cheerfully and willingly. He possessed a marvelous power over the minds of the people; they reposed unlimited faith in his sagacity, integrity, honesty and soundness of judgment. He could do almost whatever he pleased, because he never abused the confidence of the people, never betrayed their trust—because he was solely actuated by a sense of duty and patriotism.

He ever tried to do what he conscientiously believed to be right. Right was his polar star: conscience was his monitor, and he tempered all his dealings with the rebels with forbearance and mercy. He harbored no particle of animosity. He never felt the sensation of revenge in his life; he never hated a human being. His millions of admirers and friends found but one fault, and that was with his excess of lenity and kindness toward public enemies. It made his heart bleed to sign the death warrant of the worst guerilla assassin or rebel spy; he thought no evil; he wished no human being harm; he was the embodiment of Christian precepts and virtues. The Chair of State, made vacant by his death, there is none, in the land—no, not one—able to fill it as he filled it. An age produces but one Washington. Abraham Lincoln was the Washington of this generation—the second Father of his Country. In his untimely death a heavy calamity has fallen upon the American people.

———

IMPEACHMENT

May 14, 1868

THE TRIBUNE *had been characteristically vigorous in advocating the impeachment of President Johnson, and in doing so reflected the prevailing sentiment in the north. Then, two days before the senate was to reach*

*its verdict, this remarkable editorial
was published in defense of any Republican senator whose conscience
would oblige him to favor acquittal.*

*On May 16 the senate voted 35 to
19 for conviction; the change of one
vote would have given the two-thirds
majority required by the Constitution
for the removal of the President.*

There has been no more determined
opponent of Andrew Johnson in the
United States, from the day of his
defection to the present, than THE
CHICAGO TRIBUNE. This paper never
faltered nor hesitated in the condemnation of his recreancy, nor in
the exposure of his treachery and
malicious proceedings; but THE
CHICAGO TRIBUNE, in common with
a large majority of the House of
Representatives and of the Republican masses, did not see sufficient
legal grounds for an impeachment.
We opposed impeachment up to
February last, because to that time
there was no adequate legal cause
for which he could be found guilty
of high crimes and misdemeanors.
We then warned the rash, reckless
and inconsiderate, who were seeking to make "impeachment, any-
how," a policy of the party, that the
Senate could not be driven into
participation in such a proceeding,
and would resist it.

Finally, in February last, Andrew
Johnson removed the Secretary of
War and appointed a successor *ad
interim*, while the Senate was in
session, and in the excitement con-
sequent upon such a high-handed
outrage, such a bold violation of
law, and such a wanton assertion of
Executive supremacy, as it was generally regarded to be, the House of

Representatives, by a three-fourths
majority, resolved that he be impeached and brought to trial.

THE CHICAGO TRIBUNE thought
then, and thinks now, that upon
the charge of having violated the
Office-Tenure law by the removal of
Stanton and appointment of Thomas,
the Senate being at the time in
session, he had violated the law and
ought to be convicted. But the decision of that question is a judicial
one, to be decided by the High
Court provided by the constitution.
Of the fifty-four members of that
court, forty-two are Republicans. It
requires the concurrence of thirty-
six Senators to convict. Each Senator is, as to the facts and the law, a
court unto himself, to give his decision as his conscience under oath
may dictate. Certain of these Republican Senators (with all the Democrats) have announced their inability
to concur in a conviction; others
have declared their purpose to vote
for acquittal upon certain articles
and conviction upon others. These
Senators are among the most distinguished members of the Republican party—men eminent for their
statesmanship, their legal learning
and the personal purity of their
character.

THE CHICAGO TRIBUNE has not failed
in its duty in urging conviction. It
has presented to its readers all the
considerations calling for conviction. There has not been an argument of any weight, nor a reason of
a legal or of a political character
given by either of the Managers for
the conviction of Andrew Johnson,
that has not been presented in the
columns of this paper over and over

31

again. All that the case permitted to be said with fairness and truth in favor of conviction we have kept constantly before our readers.

While we have done this from an honest conviction that we were right, we have been fully aware that the case when developed in the full light of all the facts and all the law, was surrounded with difficulties and embarrassments that might fairly challenge the judgment of the noblest and the wisest. He who reads the speech of Senator Grimes, published in this paper yesterday, while differing from that Senator, cannot fail to be impressed with the remarkable nicety and fineness of the distinctions between that construction of the law which points to guilt, and that which is consistent with innocence. Strong and confirmed as are our own opinions as to the proper construction of the law, we can readily see how a man can conscientiously vote that the law means otherwise. Upon this point Senator Sherman is overwhelmed by his own record, and is forced to vote that the Office-Tenure law does not apply to Mr. Stanton as Secretary of War.

The final vote upon impeachment will not take place till Saturday. What the result may be no one can now foretell, though the possibility of a conviction still remains. But that result will not be obtained by the unanimous consent of the Republican Senators. There may be a conviction upon one, or perhaps two, articles; on the others there will be an acquittal by a vote more or less divided.

The man who demands that each Republican Senator shall blindly vote for conviction upon each article is a madman or a knave. Why a Senator, or any number of Senators, should be at liberty to vote as his conscience dictates on all the articles, provided there be a conviction on some one of them, and not be at liberty to vote conscientiously unless a conviction be secured, is only to be explained upon the theory that the President is expected to be convicted no matter whether Senators think he has been guilty or not.

We have protested, and do now protest, against the degradation and prostitution of the Republican party to an exercise of power so revolting that the people will be justified in hurling it from place at the first opportunity. We protest against any warfare by the party or any portion of it against any Senator who may, upon the final vote, feel constrained to vote against conviction upon one, several, or even all of the articles.

A conviction by a free and deliberate judgment of an honest court is the only conviction that should ever take place on impeachment; a conviction under any other circumstances will be a fatal error. To denounce such Senators as corrupt, to assail them with contumely and upbraid them with treachery for failing to understand the law in the same light as their assailants, would be unfortunate folly, to call it by the mildest term; and to attempt to drive these Senators out of the party for refusing to commit perjury, as they regard it, would cause a reaction that might prove fatal not only to the supremacy of the Republican party, but to its very existence. Those rash papers which have undertaken to ostracise Senators—men like Trumbull, Sherman, Fessenden, Grimes, Howe, Henderson, Frelinghuysen, Fowler, and others—are but aiding the Copperheads in the dismemberment of our party.

The Republican party has an immense work before it this year, in which the labors of every man of ability, influence and power will be needed. The national integrity and unity are to be made perpetual or they are to be lost. We are to place reconstruction and the national credit beyond all doubt and question by the election of a Republican President or abandon all to the Copperheads and Repudiation. We are to secure the results of the war or to sacrifice them all to folly ineffable.

In view of the magnitude of these issues the question whether Andrew Johnson, tied hand and foot, shall serve nine and a half months longer, or shall be dismissed now, sinks into insignificance. His acquittal will inflict a smart on the feelings of every Republican. But if acquitted, shall Republicans change front from the common enemy and engage in a miserable, deplorable, destructive internecine warfare with each other?

Is the party to be divided on the question of ostracizing and punishing Senators for rendering a different verdict under oath from what was hoped for? Is that to be the issue the lunatics and malignants would force upon us? Let Republicans turn their arms against the common enemy, and not against men whose personal honesty is indicated by a sacrifice to conscience far beyond the appreciation of their traducers.

Why should the failure to convict Johnson impair our strength at the coming election? Is there a man worthy of the name of Republican who desires a conviction, that purposes to vote for Pendleton, for Repudiation, for compensation for slaves, for Copperheadism and disunion, all because the High Court may acquit Johnson? Is there a man who intends to vote for Grant, who will vote for his Copperhead opponent in case Johnson is acquitted? Is the great hero of the Union cause, the savior of his country, to be held responsible for the decision of a court on a question of law? Is General Grant to be stabbed and betrayed in the house of his friends because Republicans are angry and disappointed at the decision of six or eight members of the High Court? What has Grant to do with an acquittal or conviction? How is he to

OF THE EIGHT SENATORS listed as in danger of ostracism if they voted for acquittal, five nevertheless did so. They were Fessenden of Maine, Fowler of Tennessee, Grimes of Iowa, Henderson of Missouri, and Trumbull of Illinois. The other three, Frelinghuysen of New Jersey, Howe of Wisconsin, and Sherman of Ohio voted for conviction.

In the event, Sherman was not "overwhelmed by his record" as the editor thought he would be. Sherman, during the debate on the tenure of office act, had favored exempting cabinet officers from the general rule that the President had to have the senate's permission to remove an executive official. The chief count in the impeachment was Johnson's failure to consult the senate before removing Stanton from his position as secretary of war.

GEORGE HUNT PENDLETON (1825-1889) of Ohio had been the Democratic candidate for Vice-President in 1864. At the time the editorial appeared, he was a leading candidate for the Democratic Presidential nomination. He favored redemption of government bonds in greenbacks. It is a nice question whether he was disliked by the editor more heartily on this account than for his having been McClellan's political partner. In 1869, Pendleton ran for governor of Ohio and was defeated.

33

be held accountable for the opinion of Senators in the case?

General Grant doubtless desires the removal of Johnson and will be most happy to learn that he is convicted. But we warn the incendiaries who are filling the air with cries and howls against certain Senators, that Grant will bow to the decision of the High Court, whatever it may be, and if Johnson shall not be convicted, he will take no stock in the scheme of persecution and ostracism which the mad-caps are organizing against them and lend it neither aid nor countenance. If this position of the great chieftain does not satisfy them, they can have him as a candidate, on no lower grounds.

THE OSAGE INDIAN LANDS

July 9, 1868

A prominent citizen, evidently expecting a pat on the back, receives instead a public spanking.

Mr. William Sturges, of Chicago, who is the beneficiary under the treaty with the Indians for the sale of their lands in Kansas, has written a letter, in which he gives his reasons why THE TRIBUNE should support his treaty. We fail to see that the anticipated civilization of the Indians justifies their being robbed. We should prefer that their familiarity with the habits of the white race should commence otherwise than in having their land taken from them at twenty cents an acre, when they can get $1.25 per acre for it in cash.

Mr. Sturges intimates that he has been laboring for the benefits of Chicago, and that when he builds the railroad to Galveston he will have done Chicago more good than if he had built a mile of marble stores. We do not see how the possession of the land is to build the railroad, as the purchase of the one does not require the completion of the other. If the land is so valuable beyond the price paid for it, that out of the profits Mr. Sturges proposes to build 750 miles of railway through an unbroken wilderness, then it is proof that Mr. Sturges did not pay the Indians the real value of their land. We do not think the world has progressed in morals to the extent of justifying the unlawful taking of a man's property in order to Christianize, civilize and otherwise enlighten him.

Mr. Sturges has undoubtedly felt much grief at the nomadic habits of the Indians, their want of thrift, and their general unfitness for respectable society; no one need doubt his warm interest in the prosperity of Chicago; but we fail to see that the Indians are to be civilized, the welfare of Chicago to be secured, or the character of the government of the United States, or of the American Senate to be in the least elevated, by giving validity to one of the greatest attempted land swindles which the country has heard of recently.

If these $12,000,000 worth of land are to fall into any hands besides their real owners, we suppose they may as well go to Mr. Sturges as any other. But why to anybody? Why should the government permit these Indian lands to be sold at all in this way? Why not take them and sell them for the use of the Indians to the highest bidder for actual civilization? If the Indian is to be defrauded of four-fifths of his property, let the wrong be in some other form than that of a treaty to which the United States is a contracting and a consenting party.

THE COMING WOMAN

May 15, 1870

The extension of the franchise to women became an accomplished fact half a century later, with the adoption of the 19th amendment on Aug. 26, 1920. A few long-winded paragraphs have been omitted.

Whether we like it or not—whether anybody likes it or not—it may be accepted as very nearly a foregone conclusion that the right of suffrage is eventually to be extended to women. There have been, doubtless, a great many foolish things said, and a great many more foolish things done by those who have advocated it. But when was it ever otherwise, in any reform, since Martin Luther flung his inkstand at the head of the devil; since the Roundheads gave whole texts of Scripture to their children for Christian names and denounced men who wore their hair over their shoulders as certain of eternal perdition; since such time, however remote or near, when men begin to think for themselves on any new subject, and in their new freedom, committed some extravagance, which did little harm and was soon forgotten, or, at least,

forgiven?

"Why," said Miss Anna Dickinson, on one occasion, stepping forward to the footlights and commencing a lecture with a lofty flight of eloquence, "Why was I born?" She paused, and a thrill ran through the audience. Again the rich tones of the winsome woman rolled over the expectant people, as she repeated the question, "Why was I born?" And again she paused, that the due impression might be made upon her hearers, before she answered her own question. "Why was I born?" she asked once more, in touching and almost painful accents, when a wicked boy in the gallery shouted, "I give it up!"

The incident is almost an epitome of the whole "Woman's Movement." Woman has asked a question with such solemnity as she could, and a jeer and a laugh has, for the most part, been the only answer. Oftentimes, no doubt, the ridicule has been richly deserved by individual advocates, who have shown more zeal for the cause than judgment in advocating it. But ridicule is never an argument, though it often passes for one in place of a better answer, and, for a time, seems more con-

ANNA DICKINSON (1842-1932) defies treatment in a footnote. She was regarded as among the most eloquent of the galaxy of women who preached reform at this time, and she outlived them all. As a child she wrote against slavery. She discovered her oratorical talents well before the Civil war and employed them then and later on behalf of abolition, temperance, and women's rights. During the Civil war she was used to excellent effect as a Republican speaker. Later she went on the stage, and wrote a few plays and novels. Wendell Phillips no doubt meant well when he referred to her as "the young elephant sent forward to try the bridges to see if they were safe for the older ones to cross." Sandburg writes of "her chestnut curls . . . her virginal beauty, her symmetrical figure."

clusive than the soundest reason. Reason, nevertheless, has the best of it in the long run.

The real question is, whether woman has reason on her side. When she shows that, the result is necessarily a foregone conclusion. That conclusion, probably, is already reached in the minds of most persons—that in making suffrage universal, without regard to color, condition, or intelligence, it cannot be much longer denied to that half of the body-politic who are not fools, who are not degraded, in distinction from the other half, and who differ from the rest only in sex. Once admit that representation should be universal, as a matter of right, and sex alone cannot reasonably be made a ground of exclusion.

Probably nine-tenths of those who now object to the extension of the right of suffrage to woman, object to it because they believe that suffrage should not be extended at all, but should rather be restricted, and that the governing power should be entrusted to the hands of the few— the comparatively rich, the comparatively wise, or the comparatively virtuous. But this is not the democratic doctrine; and the great majority, if not already persuaded, are fast coming to the belief that that doctrine, when carried out to its last analysis, cannot exclude woman from her fair share in self-government. The signs of the times, both in England and this country, seem to indicate this, and we may as well begin to put our houses in order for the change—if putting our houses in order is a necessity involved.

And, for our own part, we frankly acknowledge that we expect to survive it. We have been, in the course of the controversy, duly appalled and humiliated at the sad and disheartening pictures which have been so often drawn, and in such lurid colors, of the degrading spectacle of our tender mothers, and wives, and sisters, and daughters coming down into the arena of the primary meeting and the Amazonian struggle of the election day. We have been utterly confounded with the difficulty of woman properly discharging her military duty when the state shall need the services of its citizens. Our head also has ached over the problem of nursing babies and properly cooked dinners in its relations to the jury box.

We are really afraid that the wife of our bosom could not load a musket, much less fire one, and what, in that case, would become of us in a war with Great Britain, and we were compelled to stay at home and take care of the baby? Would it not be quite as badly off as the wife of our bosom with the musket and the British? These questions, and a thousand like these, have kept us awake o' nights, and thrown infinite difficulties in the way of a proper discharge of our editorial functions, especially when we have considered that presently we should be called home to attend to that other duty aforesaid, and the place that knows us now, should hereafter know some woman in our stead. Women in the editorial chair! Women at the case! Women running the engine and the press! And all these big, two-fisted fellows at home putting on diapers and washing up the tea-things!

Of course, in common with our fellow-men, we have used these arguments, and attempted to show thereby how absurd it was that women should vote, when such consequences as these must immediately and inevitably follow. But such is life. All the eloquence, on our side, has been wasted; the probable appalling results have been pointed at in vain; the women seem certainly to have got the better of us, and to have convinced, or, at least, silenced, the great majority of people, and at no very distant day we shall see the popular vote doubled, whatever may come of it. Perhaps it will not be so bad after all. At least let us hope so; let us hope that there will still be cakes and ale in the future; that woman will be woman still —the wife and the mother, the daughter and the sister, notwithstanding she has the right of saying, if she chooses, whom she would prefer for hog-reeve or Governor.

A PATERNAL GOVERNMENT

May 25, 1870

Neither the New Deal nor THE TRIB-UNE'S *distrust of it is as new as the present generation may suppose.*

The principal difference between a republican government and any other is, that its functions are limited and restrained by law to those general objects which the people cannot perform for themselves, and which of necessity, must be executed by an agent possessing the authority of all. The Constitution of the United States appoints this agent, and pre-scribes its duties and powers. Interference with the business, the liberties, or the privileges of the people, except to administer justice and perform those general duties which the people cannot perform en masse, was carefully guarded against. So strongly was the principle asserted and maintained, that, until within a very few years, the American people, outside the number who were criminals or office-holders, never experienced, practically, any interference from the National Government, and were scarcely aware of its existence except as they were called upon, once in four years, to elect a President.

There is hardly a case in history in which any body of men constituting the government, ever voluntarily laid aside prerogatives or powers once assumed. The doubtful experiment of to-day becomes the inexorable precedent of to-morrow. Men in office are forever claiming additional prerogatives, and, once allowed to exercise them, it is almost impossible for the people to recover the ground they have lost.

We have had numerous illustrations of this fact lately. Under the extraordinary circumstances of the last ten years, and the necessity of exercising extraordinary powers, there has grown up in Congress, and in the executive departments of the government, the dangerous sentiment that the government should take charge generally of the affairs of the people; not merely of their local administration, their social, moral, and educational affairs, but also the regulation of their private business, and their employments and

37

productions. The statute book already exhibits the progress made in this direction, and, of the 3,200 bills now before Congress, three-fourths propose special legislation, and interferences by the General Government in matters over which Congress and the National Government have no more legitimate jurisdiction than they have over the movement of Jupiter's satellites.

The war being over, the government and its powers, and functions, and jurisdiction have fallen back into the ordinary routine of a peace establishment. The occasion for extraordinary powers has ceased. The statesman must turn to the written charter, and there inquire what the duties of the government are. Those duties he will find to be very few and simple. He will find that it was never contemplated that the government should be the paternal institution which had existed so many centuries in other lands, and to re-establish which there is such a strong tendency among us at present. Our fathers knew the evils of such a system, and they avoided them by establishing a government whose only interference with the business and social affairs of the people was to administer justice, coin money, carry the mails, regulate our intercourse with foreign powers, and do a few other things necessary to enable us to hold the position that we can fairly earn among civilized nations.

When our government was formed, the world was active in shaking off the crust of feudalism, and we commenced the experiment of a free people governing themselves, without any interference, disturbance or direction of the government. The people were to attend each to his own affairs, and the government was to attend merely to such matters of general character as required a responsible agent. That was the kind of government which was established by the American people, who wished to escape the paternal system, then in full blast under Louis XIV in France, George III in England, and the Pope in Italy, Spain, and Austria. It was never contemplated that the people of the United States should be the children of the government, to be fed, clothed, and educated, out of their own estate by guardians; but it was intended to have a government for the execution of the laws, the preservation of order, the arbitrament of controversies among individuals, and to transact external business with other nations.

Under the paternal and patriarchal system of other days and other lands, the government built roads and canals, bridges and highways, churches and universities; it selected those who were to be soldiers and sailors, those who should be herdsmen and farmers, those who should be mechanics, and those who should be common laborers; it selected those who should be scholars and those who should be dunces, those who should marry and those who should not; those who should be priests and those who should be laymen, those who should be nobles and those who should be plebeians. It regulated the hours of labor and the compensation therefor. It prescribed who should be workers in gold and who in iron, who should cultivate the soil, and what crops and how much should be raised, and what kind of cattle should be bred. It regulated the price of food, the length of the hair, the quality of the clothing, and the shape of buttons. It required a special license to smoke, to fish, to hunt, or to own a horse or vehicle. It regulated the hours of rising and of going to bed, and the time to be devoted to religion and the form of the prayers to be used, and the kind of faggots that heretics should be burned with. It governed the people as the father governs the infants of his family, and endeavored to teach them that all the blessings of life were due to the sovereign wisdom, bounty, and clemency of the government.

With the close of the war, during which so many unwonted powers were exercised, the theory of paternal government has been revived among us. Perhaps nobody in particular is to blame, but so firmly has it become rooted that almost everybody who is not prosperous in business rushes to Congress for relief, or writes to his Representative that something ought to be done to help him. It is expected that government shall build steamboats and railways, and hire people to operate them; construct bridges, dig out harbors, rivers, and canals; regulate the hours of labor, provide compulsory education, teach men mechanic arts, give bounties to particular industries, and levy taxes upon other industries; prohibit certain kinds of importations and exportations, and encourage other kinds; prescribe what persons shall be admitted to hotels, theatres, and restaurants,

and generally make itself a hateful and costly nuisance. Congress, nothing loath to find its powers and jurisdiction enlarged, sets forth confidently to bring in the millennium. The only means which it has at command is the power to tax. If railroads, steamboats, canals, rivers, harbors, universities, manufactures, mines, navigation, etc., are to be promoted and "fostered" by the government, it can only be done by the proceeds of taxes, for the government does not derive its revenue from the prayers of the faithful. Whatever it gives to one it must take from another. So the taxes are imposed, and the proceeds distributed. This is the paternal government of the feudal system, modified only by religious toleration. How long we shall enjoy this single exemption it is, perhaps, not safe to predict.

———

SHALL THE SWORD SUPERSEDE THE LAW?

April 18, 1871

Amid the excesses of the Reconstruction era, the Editor raises his voice in defense of civil liberty and against military rule.

The Force act of April 20, 1871 was adopted for the ostensible purpose of suppressing the original Ku Klux Klan. (In all probability the organization insofar as it recognized Gen. Nathan Bedford Forrest as its leader, had already been disbanded by him in 1869.) The unstated purpose of the act was to prolong the carpetbag era in the south. The grant of authority to suspend the writ of habeas corpus was used only once, on Oct. 17, 1871,

39

in nine counties of South Carolina. In 1882 the Supreme court declared the law unconstitutional.

Popular governments cannot be maintained by the sword. Insurrections, rebellions, disorders, and personal violations of law may be suppressed by the vigorous application of military force, but the real strength and defence of popular governments is the law which is enforced by popular sentiment. The very theory upon which free governments rest is, that they exist by the consent of the governed.

The American people, in forming their government, substituted popular representation and the right, under certain restrictions, to change the constitution at their pleasure, in the place of forcible revolution; but nowhere have they ever abandoned the principle that the government is one of law, and that force was only to be used in aid of law, to execute it, not to destroy it. When the time shall come that a government of law shall be done away with; when a Brigadier General shall be installed as the maker of law, and his Quartermaster, Paymaster, and Commissary shall become the supreme justiciary of each State; and Colonels, Majors, and Captains shall exercise the functions of civil officers, and sergeants and corporals shall be the Sheriffs and police; when the writ of habeas corpus shall be prohibited, the trial by jury abolished; when the laws shall be found in "general orders" instead of the statute book, and the only form of justice shall be the proceedings of courts-martial—then popular government may be said to have ceased, and the despotism of the bayonet erected in its place.

Have the American people so retrograded in intelligence, and respect for the law, that it is necessary to set aside the constitution and the statute book, the executive, judicial, and municipal officers of the people, and to provide that the President, at any moment, upon his own motion, and at his own discretion, may enter any State, declare martial law, suspend civil authority, and make a military commander sole arbiter in all matters of life, property, and liberty? Has popular government so far proved a failure that, in the most profound peace, when there is not in all the broad land an organized force opposing the Federal laws, or questioning Federal authority, the Congress of the United States should provide for a military despotism to take the place of the government chosen by the popular will and existing by the popular consent?

What is there in the condition of the State of Illinois which justifies the suspicion of such intolerable anarchy, and warrants the substitution of armed force for the civil law? Yet both houses of Congress have passed just such a bill, and are only divided as to some of the details. Both houses have agreed to place in the hands of the President this unexampled power, wholly unwarranted by the constitution, and only defensible upon the plea that free government is a failure, that popular intelligence has been perverted, and that to the army is to be committed the task of averting general anarchy. Against this grave assumption we protest; and we trust that, upon the reassembling of Con-

40

gress in December, this law, so sweeping in its assumptions, and so dangerous as a precedent, may be repealed by an unanimous vote, and that meanwhile the dangerous powers it seeks to confer may not be exercised.

REBUILD THE CITY

October 12, 1871

The Chicago fire began on the night of Oct. 8, 1871. THE TRIBUNE *plant was destroyed. The paper resumed publication on Oct. 12.*

All is not lost. Though four hundred million dollars' worth of property has been destroyed, Chicago still exists. She was not a mere collection of stone, and bricks, and lumber. These were but the evidence of the power which produced these things; they were but the external proof of the high courage, unconquerable energy, strong faith, and restless perseverance which have built up here a commercial metropolis. The great natural resources are all in existence; the lake, with its navies, the spacious harbor, the vast empire of production, extending westward to the Pacific; the great outlet from the lakes to the ocean, the thirty-six lines of railways connecting the city with every part of the continent—these, the great arteries of trade and commerce, all remain unimpaired, undiminished, and all ready for immediate resumption.

What, therefore, has been lost? We have lost the accumulated profits of twenty years of prosperous growth. We have lost the stock in trade on hand on the night of the fire. We have lost money—but we have saved life, health, vigor, and industry. We have a dozen grain elevators yet remaining. We have the material on hand with which to replace those which we have lost. We have, within 36 hours' time, the whole country to draw upon for supplies of every description of goods. In two weeks from the date of the fire our merchants can fill almost any order for merchandise that may be sent them. The credit of Chicago is saved. When the whole country has faith, and hope, and confidence in us, there will be no depression in Chicago itself. The wholesale trade of the city can be resumed at once. Temporary warehouses are being erected, and business resumed.

Let no trouble be borrowed from the past. All the losses of the fire, will in time be passed into the great clearing house, and the payment of balances will be made easy for everybody. Rich men have become poor; the accumulations of years have been destroyed; but no one will sit down and waste time crying for spilled milk. Labor will be resumed. Production will be restored, and the general trade and commerce of the city will at once be resumed.

Let us avail ourselves of the liberal spirit which the country has shown in our calamity. There are no relentless creditors pressing us for payment, foreclosing mortgages, or demanding the full measure of their bonds. On the contrary, the world is asking us to take money,—unlimited credit, and go ahead, leaving the past to be taken care of in the future, when Chicago shall have resumed her power and glory.

Let the watchword henceforth be: *Chicago Shall Rise Again.*

WHY THE COMMUNE IS POSSIBLE IN AMERICA

May 24, 1874

There was Communist agitation in America 70 years ago. Here is an early attempt to appraise the movement.

The First International was organized by Karl Marx in Europe in 1864. The headquarters were moved to America in 1872. The organization dissolved after the Philadelphia conference of 1876.

Note the remarks on the tariff. THE TRIBUNE, *in contrast to many eastern Republican newspapers, has not been an advocate of high protection.*

An attempt to organize the Commune presupposes a peculiar mental or moral state. A man, in order to try it, must believe the jingling lie that property is robbery, or he must think that every two-legged animal without feathers has a natural right to be a law unto himself, and to act exactly as he wishes. Very many Americans believe these two things already, and we, as a nation, are perhaps drifting towards that belief.

Take the required mental state. The supply of quantities of irredeemable shinplasters is boldly advocated by many political leaders in speeches that are, in some cases unconsciously, based on the maxim that property is robbery. More greenbacks, they say, will make money cheap. That is, they will make it possible to pay debts with less value. In other words, cheating his creditors will be put within the debtor's power. This reduces property-robbery to practice.

The tariff, again, is supported, in papers and platforms, by the plea that it gives employment to skilled workmen. This implies that it is the duty of the State to give them employment. If this is so no valid objection can be urged against the plea that it is also its duty to provide work for the unskilled. The crowds that demanded employment, last winter, of the civic authorities in New York, Boston, Cincinnati, and Chicago, were but the complement of the majorities that have passed the high-tariff bills through Congress. The constituents were but carrying the Congressmen's arguments to their legitimate conclusion. Now this is but the maxim: "Property is robbery" put into practice. For if every man has a right to his own, neither he nor his representative, the State, can justly be called upon to share his property with another man who happens to be in need.

Our tendency towards the Commune is accelerated by four main causes. The growing disbelief in creeds that were formulated centuries ago induces thinkers to try to formulate new ones, adapted to this age, but leads the careless into contemptuous rejection of all the ideas, moral and otherwise, on which the old creeds were based. It is characteristic of ignorance to go to extremes.

In the second place, the momentary triumph of the Commune in Paris, and its struggles elsewhere in Europe, have drawn attention to the subject. It is said that Berlin workingmen agreed to proclaim the Commune at the same time with their Parisian fellows, and were only prevented from doing so by the untimely discovery of their plot. The red flag waves now in the clubrooms of the German "Social-Democrats," and their daily greeting is: "Wie gehts mit der Theilung?"—"How goes it with the division (of property)?" After a thing has failed it is very easy to think you see why. No doubt the reasons of the collapse of the Paris Commune have been conned over in thousands of brains. Men imagine they could carry through such a scheme now, and are impatient to try.

Again, the great influx of foreigners has implanted on American soil the ideas that have been the outgrowth of centuries of European want, woe, and wrong. The circumstances here are not as favorable to their growth, but they grow nevertheless. The leaven is at work. It may yet leaven the whole lump.

And, finally, the growing gulf between rich and poor, the sharply-marked division between the two in a country in which cash and caste are apt to be cause and effect,—this is creating a social stratification in which the lowest stratum is volcanic, is boiling over with hate of its condition and rage at those above it. When this is the case look out for an explosion. It is not strange that a workingman, sitting in an undrained, unsunned tenement on a back-alley, should bitterly contrast his fate with that of his employer and argue: "I am as good a man as he; why should he have everything and I nothing? Why should not my mates and I seize upon the houses, the furniture, the food he has bought with the product of our labor? Might makes right. There is no militia to meet us. Hurrah for the Commune!" Such vague gropings after reason, if acted upon, would put the wealth of any large city into the hands of the poor ere nightfall to-day.

The growing tendency must be checked. There is but one way to do this. The workingman must be given comfort, mental and physical. Put sewers in every street and you check crime and communism. Ventilate every house and you check them again. Build schoolhouses and fill them by compulsion, if need be; put knowledge, by cheap lectures, and museums, and public libraries— libraries set in the heart of districts in which poverty lives—within the reach of young and old; secure the workingman a larger share in the product of his labor by encouraging co-operation, and you make the Commune impossible. We cannot wash our hands of this matter. If we do we sow the wind and leave our children to reap the whirlwind. "After us the deluge" is a neatly-sounding phrase compared with "After the Commune."

TO THE READERS OF THE TRIBUNE

November 9, 1874

Joseph Medill announces his resumption of control of THE TRIBUNE *and his program for its development.*

With this issue of THE TRIBUNE I resume its editorial control. Having within the past fortnight purchased enough shares, added to what I previously owned, to constitute a majority of the stock, the responsibility of the future management of THE TRIBUNE will necessarily devolve on me. With what degree of ability and success I shall discharge the new obligations, time alone can make known—for "Let not him boast who putteth on his armor, but rather him who taketh it off." A few words of explanation may not be inappropriate in this connection.

Shortly after the close of the Great Rebellion I was obliged by ill-health, caused by overwork, to resign the Managing Editorship of THE TRIBUNE, first to the late Dr. C. H. Ray, and, after he vacated his post, to Mr. Horace White, who has since then had chief control of the paper. After a brief rest I took an editorial chair and wrote for its columns for several years. At first the political course of THE TRIBUNE, under the new management, received my approval in the main; but questions began to arise about which we sharply differed. Both being men tenacious of their opinions, it was difficult to harmonize our conflicting views and agree as to the course THE TRIBUNE should pursue. Those disagreements became more irreconcilable as the paper drifted away from the Republican party and approached the position of an Opposition journal. Finding myself circumscribed within a gradually narrowing circle of topics in which we were in accord, I retired altogether from the editorial columns of THE TRIBUNE. Our differences, however, were always political, and not personal.

My predecessor has pursued the course which he believed to be the path of duty with a courage which challenged the respect of those who condemned it, and supported his views with an ability which extorted their admiration; and he leaves his editorial chair after having achieved a national reputation.

The readers of THE TRIBUNE will naturally desire to be informed, at the outset, of the probable line of conduct of THE TRIBUNE under the change of management. A full explanation cannot be given on the instant. Men's opinions and actions are more or less influenced and controlled by the circumstances which surround them, and always by unforeseen causes. But this much may now be safely promised: THE TRIBUNE hereafter will be, as it formerly was, when under my direction, an independent Republican journal. It will be the organ of no man, however high; no clique or ring, however influential; or faction, however fanatical or demonstrative. While giving to the Republican party and its principles a hearty and generous support, it will criticise the actions and records of Republican leaders as freely and fearlessly as in days of yore. But it has seemed to me unwise for a great representative journal, for the purpose of correcting some alleged abuses of administration, to desert its party organization and turn its guns on its old friends, or help into power and place the leaders of the organization whose political records and whose official conduct show that they are insincere in their professions of desire for administrative purification.

44

As a general rule, a man can exercise more influence for good among his friends by remaining *en rapport* with than by assailing and traducing them. The same rule holds true in regard to newspapers. The Government of the Nation must be conducted through the instrumentality of parties. I know of no other agency which has succeeded in free countries. The party in the majority must assume the responsibility of governing. A party is simply a voluntary organization of citizens united to carry into effect certain principles and purposes. It must employ and intrust individuals to collect and disburse taxes, to perform executive and police duties for protection and security of person and property; men must be engaged to construct public works, carry the mails, administer justice, and make and execute laws, and do a thousand other things which the public well-being requires; and these individuals will often prove careless, inefficient, or corrupt. But a party whose aims and purposes are good and patriotic, and whose record is grand and glorious, should not be condemned and thrown out of power on account of the defective work or misconduct of a few of its employes, in order to make place for an antagonistic organization whose record cannot be defended, but is regarded with sorrow and shame by its best members, and whose conduct when in power never fails to show that its reformatory professions when out of power are a delusion and a snare.

Such being the case in regard to the necessity and machinery of parties in free countries, the Press, to be useful, cannot avoid being partisan in greater or less degree. If an editor undertakes the *role* of supporting both sides, his position is equivalent to a double affirmative, which amounts to a negative. If he habitually censures and condemns both, he is soon regarded as a common scold and a nuisance. To be entirely unpartisan leaves him in the condition of a cipher; and when a newspaper undertakes to be wholly "independent" of its party and yet discuss politics, it is on the high road to the camp of its political opponents, whether its conductor so intended at the outset or not—unless, indeed he takes refuge in the coward's harbor of neutrality and abdicates his duties altogether, which is a most contemptible and despicable position. But it is not essential to the prosperity or influence of a party paper that it should willfully misrepresent its opponents, and behold nothing but evil and depravity in all their actions, or discover only treasonable designs in all they propose to do. Candor and fairness in the treatment of political opponents will detract nothing from the influence of a paper, nor will it injure the prospects of its own party.

Such, in brief, are the views I have long entertained of parties, and the relations which the Press should bear towards them. A political newspaper, to be of service to the public, must give one party or the other the preference. And, while the Democratic party embraces many excellent and worthy members, who would be an honor to any organization, yet I sincerely believe the Republican party comprises a much larger proportion of the intelligent and educated classes, of the moral worth and business enterprise, as well as of the patriotic elements, of the nation; and therefore the Government of the country and the civil rights of the poor and weak can be more safely and prudently committed to its keeping than to that of its antagonist, whose past history and antecedents furnish so much cause for misgivings and dread of its future behavior.

Looking, then, at the individual composition of the two great parties —all other parties being mere fragments, ephemeral in duration and narrow in object—and at their respective records and underlying principles, I cannot hesitate to give the decided preference to the Republican party. Hence, THE TRIBUNE will be conducted as a Republican journal.

Having said this much in a general way, it only remains to be added, that no labor or expense will be spared to keep THE TRIBUNE in the very front ranks of journalism as a *news*-paper in all departments of current intelligence and activity. The high position it has attained as an advocate of the material, moral, and intellectual progress of the people, will be maintained and advanced as far as possible. It will be my constant aim and endeavor to make THE TRIBUNE not only a welcome but useful visitor to the fireside, as well as to the counting-room, shop, and office.

For the cordial greeting with which the brethren of the Press have welcomed me back to the editorial arena, I tender them my most heartfelt acknowledgments, and, for the hundreds of congratulatory letters and telegrams received from old friends, they have my sincere thanks for their kind expressions and good wishes. Respectfully,

J. Medill

THE HAPPY OUTLOOK

February 18, 1877

The danger which confronted the nation as a result of the contested election of 1876 is made clear in this editorial. The dispute was referred for decision to a commission composed of five senators, five representatives, and five justices of the Supreme court. The vote was 8 to 7 for Hayes.

The American people have reason this morning for thanks that the Presidential election has been settled. We make no difference between Democrats and Republicans,—both have equal cause for rejoicing that the angry contest has been closed. We do not claim that this national gratitude is due because Hayes is declared elected; it would have been equally due had Tilden received the award. This gratitude is due that a controversy of such universal interest—one upon which the whole American people have been so earnestly and so equally divided; which has engrossed the excited attention of every city, town, hamlet, household, and person in the land—has been terminated by the peaceful judgment of a court of law. Never in the history of the country, never in the history of any people in any age, has there been a braver, nobler vindication and example of unconquerable devotion to the wise and peaceful decrees of the courts of law. Now, more than ever before, have the American people shown their ability to conquer their own partisanship, and yield all their prejudices and convictions to the decision of the constituted legal authorities. Over all this broad land there is today a peaceful acceptance and acquiescence in the judgment of the Court; violence is overcome, resistance withdrawn, the threat of civil war is silenced; and the spirit of insubordination and revenge finds expression only in the determination to reverse this decision at the election in 1880.

To fully appreciate the condition of the country today, as the result of this arbitration, it is only necessary to recall the circumstances under which the arbitration law was passed. At that time, and for weeks previously, the extreme partisans of both parties had determined to have their men declared elected at all hazards. Tilden had 184 votes, and Hayes had 184 votes, and the two were claimants for the odd vote in Oregon. This vote in Oregon was contested, as were the 4 votes in Florida and the 8 votes in Louisiana. Each candidate had, officially certified, 184 votes, excluding one vote of Oregon. The President of the Senate was a Republican. The House of Representatives had a large Democratic majority. The House denied the power to count the vote of any State, without the concurrence of both Houses, and, under this claim, proposed to object to counting the certified votes of Florida and Louisi-

ana, and, thereupon assuming that neither candidate had a majority, proposed to proceed at once to an election of President. On the other hand, it was claimed that the Republican President of the Senate, having the custody and possession of the certificates of votes, should proceed to count the votes, deciding that the Republican votes from Louisiana, Florida, and Oregon should alone be considered. Whereupon, he was to count Hayes in, and officially declare him elected President.

Between these two antagonizing parties was a body of Republicans who did not believe, and who would not be coerced into approving, that the President of the Senate had any judicial powers, and therefore could not lawfully undertake to decide questions of law and of fact between opposing claims; that his powers were merely ministerial, which any clerk could execute as well as he could. There were also Democrats who did not approve the doctrine that either House could veto the counting of the vote of a State, without the concurrence of the other House, and, therefore, that the proposed action of the House in electing President by a call of the States would be revolutionary. Behind all these was the vast army of office-seekers and officeholders, clamorous for whatever action would give them a hope or promise of being pensioned on the Government.

Both parties were being precipitated into rash and revolutionary measures. Both were wrong. Both claimed powers which were outside of the Constitution, and which were indefensible. Both were rushing to a formal declaration of the election of President by unconstitutional action. Each party had "the game in its own hands," from a party point of view, and each was preparing to make sure of that game. The result was inevitable. On the day fixed for counting the votes—the 14th of February—there would have been two Presidents declared elected; and today, from Maine to Texas, from Florida to far-off Oregon, men would be busy preparing for the arbitrament of power by force.

The people of Louisiana would by this time be cutting throats, and the long-restrained passion for a war of races would be let loose. The State Governments of the other fifteen States of the South would be at the service of Tilden to support his Presidency. Oregon, Connecticut, New York, New Jersey, and Indiana, would all recognize and espouse, through their Executives, the cause of Tilden. The House of Representatives—the immediate representatives of the people and one branch of Congress—would recognize Tilden as the lawfully chosen President. On the other hand, the majority in the Senate would recognize Hayes and oppose Tilden. The other seventeen Northern States, being in the control of Republican Governments, would all recognize Hayes, and would support him.

In each State there would be a minority, nearly as numerous as the majority, in violent opposition to the State Government and in support of the adverse President. Local elections all over the country would turn on the election of officers supporting Tilden or Hayes. It would not be three months before the whole country would be in all the blaze and fury of bitter, malicious civil war. Law and authority would be paralyzed. Crime would enlist under the banners of the opposing forces, and life and property would share the consequences of anarchy. Business would be at an end. Riots and plunder would be general; and all for the want of an authorized tribunal to decide a question of law.

Instead of this horrible condition of affairs, we have today, in the judgment of this Court of Arbitration, the peaceful, legal determination of the whole controversy. We have escaped the revolutionary election of Tilden by the House of Representatives, and the revolutionary election of Hayes by the President of the Senate. We have escaped the calamity of the election of two Presidents, and a divided Congress and a divided country on that subject. We have escaped political disorder and confusion, paralyzation of the Government, and the substitution of anarchy for law. We have secured peace. We have erected law, and to the decision of the law the whole country submits, and the nation moves on as safely and securely as if no danger had threatened its peace and stability.

Under the circumstances of a peaceful and united country, as the result of this arbitration, the indignant declarations of the Democrats and Republicans who a few weeks ago were shouting, "We wash our hands of all responsibility for this measure," appear in all their criminal stupidity, and the American people who are not office-holders or office-seekers have cause to thank the wisdom and the patriotism of the men who devised this scheme of peace and union, and the supremacy of law.

————

OFFICE-BEGGING

February 25, 1877

One of many editorials in favor of reforming the civil service. This one was chosen for its concise description of the patronage methods of the time; and also, let it be confessed, to rescue from oblivion the monumental joke played on Mr. Speaker in '69.

The office-beggars have begun their work. The legislative halls at Springfield are infested with the men with petitions asking signatures to appeals to President Hayes for office. We notice even that a caucus has been called to decide who of all the Republicans of Illinois shall be selected by the President for a place in his Cabinet, and which place shall be assigned to the representative of this State.

With the fatality of all such caucuses, the probability is that the caucus will select some one man for some particular place, and will, according to precedent, declare that no other man in Illinois shall be selected for a place in the Cabinet, or for any other than the place designated. Gov. Hayes in all probability will select his Cabinet from public men with whose record and history he is acquainted, and who will not need petitions and resolutions to make him aware of their fitness and ability.

It being understood that the Legislative caucus will have but one choice of office in the Cabinet, and but one person to fill that particular office, all the other aspirants are compelled to seek minor places. Thus, petitions are in circulation recommending men for Collector of Customs, Collector of Internal Revenue, Marshal, and Postmaster, in Chicago, and also for subordinate places under these officers. The value of these petitions, or their want of value, was happily illustrated in 1869, when a memorial was addressed to President Grant asking that the gentleman who was then Speaker of the House in the General Assembly be arrested, and for his various crimes, all enumerated, he be forever banished the United States and denied the privilege of claiming to be an American citizen. This petition was signed by all the members of the General Assembly, and conspicuously and officially by the gentleman whose banishment was asked.

These office-begging papers are evidence more than anything else of the utter pauperism of the supplicants. They are generally signed without objection, for the same reason that a man gives a dime to and hurries away from the mendicant who offers to make profert of his putridity. Still, the disgraceful business is going on at Springfield, and before the Legislature adjourns they will have recommended to the new President not only enough persons to fill all the Federal offices in this State, but also to supply a complete new force to fill the diplomatic corps.

It would be well for these office-beggars to read over what Gov. Hayes said on this subject of appointments and removals from office, in his letter of acceptance, and also that part of the Republican platform adopted at Cincinnati on the same subject. Both of these documents are instructive reading just at this time, when a President is about to be inaugurated who declared that he would not accept a second term, so that he might be independent and free in his purpose to reform the civil service, especially in the matter of removals and appointments. Petitions for office, even for Cabinet offices, are not likely to have much weight with a President who does not propose to make changes for change sake, nor to overlook the points of capacity and integrity on the part of the persons to be appointed.

———

"HARD TIMES" AND THE RAILROADS

July 24, 1878

Jay Cooke, who popularized bond selling during the Civil war, emerged as the country's leading banker. His banks became over-extended in financing the Northern Pacific railroad. Cooke later retrieved his losses by investments in mines. Here is a penetrating analysis of the circumstances of the panic of 1873 precipitated by Cooke's failure. Note the clear understanding of the importance in the business cycle of credit expansion and investment in capital goods.

The revival of Jay Cooke's bankrupt affairs for the moment calls to mind one of the greatest and most disastrous causes of the panic and the long era of depression that has followed. The collapse of Jay Cooke & Company was merely a signal—a sort of an alarm-bell—that roused the country to an apprehension of what was coming. The history of what followed is too familiar and too disagreeable to dwell upon; we are still in the toils, after five years of depression and suffering, and people are still wondering what brought it all about.

It wasn't merely a "loss of confidence," because it doesn't require five years for an intelligent people to recover from a fright. It wasn't altogether the depreciated condition of the currency, for the currency, though exerting a baleful influence on business pending the process of squeezing out the water, has for some time been practically at par with coin, and was worth 88 per cent at the time of the panic. It wasn't any deficiency in the amount of currency, because, ever since the panic, money has been more abundant and obtainable at lower rates than ever before. In spite of all the wisdom that has been uttered about hard times, and in spite of the discussion that is constantly kept up, the one great cause is either overlooked altogether or underestimated. Jay Cooke's affairs recall it, for Jay Cooke was in the railroad business.

During the four years of the War there was ample employment for all classes of people. A million men on one side were engaged in cutting the throats of half a million or more on the other. The remainder of the population was employed at high wages or large profits; money and speculation were abundant, for the

Government was mortgaging the future and spending the proceeds at the rate of three millions a day.

The War ended in April, 1865, and the vast armies were thrown out of Government employment; more than this, immigration, which had dwindled down small during the War, revived, and fleets of ships were bringing foreigners to this country in search of employment by hundreds of thousands. There was no complaint about lack of work or insufficient wages,—no hard times. Everything went forward in a booming fashion; the armies from the battle-fields of the South, and the other vast armies from Europe pouring in upon us, found no difficulty in locating themselves satisfactorily.

What became of all these people? What supported them? Why, we went on mortgaging the future for more money just as we had done during the War, and spent it just as lavishly. The Government was no longer the agent who negotiated the funds; corporations stepped in and acted as distributing agents. The Government had borrowed some $2,800,000,000 during five years. The corporations borrowed more than double that amount during the next eight years.

Of the latter, the railroad companies were the most numerous, powerful, and hazardous. The latest statistics show the railroad debt of the country to be nearly five billions ($4,806,202,022), including stock, bonds, and floating indebtedness, or nearly double the highest figure the Government debt ever reached. More than half of this money was raised and expended within the period between the close of the War in '65, and the panic in '73, dating from Jay Cooke's collapse. During this period nearly forty thousand miles of railway was constructed.

The business of building railroads on a grand scale is the largest manufacturing business that can be conceived. It is no exaggeration to say that, directly or indirectly, railroad-building employed more than a million men during the period to which we refer. The great trans-continental route was pushed through with a rapidity altogether unparalleled, driving Indians and buffaloes before it. The Western States passed laws allowing cities, towns, and counties to mortgage themselves to their heart's content for the construction of new railroads, and the whole country was grid-ironed over with tracks. On the old roads single tracks were increased to double tracks, and double tracks to quadruple tracks; iron rails were taken up to give way to steel rails; connections, extensions and offshoots were provided in every direction. Along the line of the new roads the carpenter and builder followed closely upon the first run of the locomotive, and new towns sprang up like mushrooms in the night.

All this was giving employment for the time being at high wages to tens of thousands. There were the machine and car shops to build; there were the iron-furnaces, foundries, and rolling-mills to run; there was coal and iron to mine and transport, the timber to cut, the road-bed, deep cuts, fills, and tunnels to make, and the bridges to build; there were the rails to cast and to lay, the

51

thousands of locomotives and hundreds of thousands of cars to construct; there was constantly a new country to open and settle, with the manifold employments incident thereto. All this was one vast manufacturing interest, and money was pouring in from abroad to carry it on with unexampled vigor. There was no lack of employment then, no complaint of low wages, no suffering from hard times.

But this gigantic industry came to a sudden standstill when the panic struck it. A general halt was called all along the line. The capitalists of Europe who had been so lavish and confident suddenly cut short the money-supply. They had suffered losses abroad, and began to tremble for their American investments. The work of building railroads may be said to have ceased as a great, national industry. Since 1873 it has consisted mainly of filling up gaps, and furnishing with termini the mass of railroads that began and ended nowhere.

But the general suspension of work, necessitated by the inability to raise any more money for unproductive railroad-building, threw out of employment hundreds of thousands of men. The furnaces were blown out, the mills shut down, work on new roads abandoned, and the building of new towns indefinitely postponed. During the years succeeding the virtual collapse of the great railroad industry, the hundreds of thousands thereby thrown out of employment have been crowding against those employed in other pursuits and against each other, and they have broken

the labor market and kept it down. Meanwhile, of course, other important influences have contributed to the general distress; but they have been cumulative, while the shock from the general collapse of railroad-building was the fundamental cause of the hard times from which we have not yet recovered.

THE AGE OF IRON

August 4, 1879

Historians fix the summer of 1879 as the beginning of recovery from the economic crisis of the '70s. This editorial was a prompt recognition of the turn. The importance of steel as a barometer of industrial prosperity is emphasized. Ida Tarbell, who in Volume IX of "A History of America" covered the period 1878-1898, says that THE TRIBUNE in this period was already firmly established as one of the newspapers "best informed on economic subjects."

This is the age of iron, and the revival of iron industries throughout the country means that the hard times period is passed. Bottom prices have been reached; the turn has been made, and we are on the up-grade. No more sound merchants will fail; no more factories will come under the hammer of the auctioneer; the fashion of failing in business has gone out, and the fashion of succeeding has come in.

The revival of prosperity in the iron trade is an unfailing sign of the revival of all other industries. Iron, in its varied forms, may be said to enter into everything in the modern world of manufacture, from the

52

needle of the seamstress to the huge steamship—"the monarch of the sea." Railways consume vast quantities of it; the manufacturers of agricultural implements take thousands of tons; it goes into millions of sewing-machines, in delicately-wrought .shapes, and into hotels and warehouses in the form of huge columns, beams, and rafters. It constitutes a part of every mill, factory, shop, and warehouse in the land.

Extracted from the bowels of the earth in its crude form, it is manipulated in the foundry and work-shop, and sent back to the mouth of the pit, where, with the aid of steam, it drags to the surface ponderous loads of ore, to be in its turn converted to the use of man. Iron glows red-hot in the kitchen-stove, and is found hidden away beneath the rich upholstery of the comfortable arm-chair in the drawing-room; the horse that trots a mile in two minutes and a quarter is shod with it, and the locomotive that draws hundreds of tons and makes forty miles an hour is made of it.

Iron is the universal necessity of man, the Alpha and Omega of material progress. To realize how essential it is to every common art, we have only to imagine, if we can, a world deprived of it,—no rail, no telegraph, no steamship, no sewing-machines, no looms, no spindles, no factory. What, then, would become of all the stalwart and the cunning workers in iron? The world would be darker than it was in the middle ages. To supply the comforts and luxuries we now have would require all mankind to labor, not eight, but sixteen hours a day.

When it is said that "Furnaces that have been idle for years are being put in blast"; that "Rolling mills are running night and day"; that "There is a rapid advance in prices of iron"; that "Every manufacturer of railway supplies has more orders than he can fill"; and, finally, that the "boom" is so pronounced that "All the mills have sent out circulars advancing prices," —when these are found to be the conditions of the iron market and the iron industry, a decided improvement in every department of labor and trade may be expected soon to follow. It is quite impossible that the iron-workers should prosper without stimulating every other industry and promoting the healthful growth of every department of trade.

And there is good reason to believe that this result has been already attained. From 1873 to 1878, inclusive, there was a steady decline in prices of all commodities. Each year the merchant, when he "took stock," was obliged to record a loss of from 10 to 20 per cent. In most cases, this steady decline for five years "wiped out" the profit side of the trial-balance; and in thousands of cases it did more, Bankruptcy Court. With the resumption of specie-payments, this decline in values generally ceased. In 1879 the mercantile class entered upon the year's business without fear of the shrinkage of stocks, and the first half of the year shows no shrinkage. On the contrary, there has been a slight advance in the price of many commodities.

53

Of course Mr. Congressman Wright's Depression Committee have taken no notice of this healthful sign; nor have they observed the indubitable evidences of a grand revival in the iron industries of the country. None are so blind as those who refuse to see. Wright is junketing at the expense of taxpayers, and junketing with a purpose. He is courting Socialists, Communists, and Fiatists, and it is from these classes that he seeks and obtains testimony.

The Democratic party is not ready for prosperous times. The Presidential campaign of 1880 impends, and Wright is in pursuit of evidence to prove that resumption, brought about by the Republican party, has not brought prosperity. But he is too late. The "boom" of the iron industries will overwhelm Democrats, Communists, Socialists, and Fiatists in one common ruin. The country is on the high road to prosperity, and, before the Presidential Convention of 1880 shall have been held, the present strong indications of a general revival of business will have crystallized into an active commercial and industrial campaign. The Socialists and the Communists —the rank and file—will have found constant employment; and they will have no time to listen to the wild and foolish harangues of their demagogical leaders. Make way for the iron horse!

HENDRICK B. WRIGHT (1808-1881) was a Pennsylvania Democrat whose congressional career began in 1855 and continued, with some interruptions, until the year of his death. At the time this editorial was written he was chairman of the Labor committee which was traveling about the country, taking testimony. The hearing in Chicago had opened on July 29 and was concluded on Aug. 2, two days before the editorial appeared.

MR. EDISON'S BACKBITERS

January 15, 1880

Edison invented the incandescent lamp on Oct. 21, 1879.

The name of the gentleman from Detroit whose observations provoked this editorial is unknown.

It is an envious world, my masters. It is full of jealousy. These two qualities, or rather malignities,—for they are the meanest manifestations of which human nature is capable,— seem to have no limit to their development. They are found in all ranks of society and in all departments of labor. If a singer succeeds in a certain part, there will always be other singers who will declare not only that she did not succeed, but that she cannot sing at all, for the reason that she has done what the others cannot do. This is a fair illustration of the general operation of envy. If the backbiter could accomplish what the other has, it would be accomplished, but, not being able to do so, all merit is denied. There are very few persons in the world who have achieved success, obtained stations of prominence, or conferred real benefit upon the world, who have not suffered from this invidiousness and have not had to fight their way through a legion of envious detractors. Among these no one has suffered more than Mr. Edison.

When, after months of quiet, patient, exhaustive labor, Mr. Edison announced his belief that he had solved the problem of the electric light, the backbiters at once commenced their work, without even waiting for him to explain the *modus*

54

operandi of his processes, or even having the courtesy to abide the results of his experiments, which he announced would publicly take place, and to which they had free access. One prominent electrician declared that the new lamp was a fraud because it would not burn, and he knew, because he had applied the same principle and it did not succeed; hence, Edison's lamp could not; but it did. The lamp burned. Another declared that the lamp might burn, but it wouldn't burn over an hour, because his didn't; but Mr. Edison's lamp has been burning day in and day out, and it still burns. Still another declared that the lamp couldn't burn, because the oxygen would enter it where the wires connect, as it did with his; but the oxygen did not enter where the wires connect, consequently the carbonized horseshoe did not crumble out of sight, as Mr. Edison's invidious rival said it would.

Now comes still another in Detroit, the agent of a rival electric light, who seeks to strip Mr. Edison of all credit, not only for his light but for many of his past inventions which have already proved of benefit to the world and have been acknowledged as successful. This latest carper, eager to advertise his own wares, declares that nothing which Mr. Edison claims belongs to him; that his original use of platinum, his later use of carbon, his application of the non-conductibility of the latter, his exhaustion of the air in the lamp, and his use of the generator are all borrowed, consequently Mr. Edison's lamp cannot succeed, and no other can, except that for which he is agent. It is somewhat remarkable that this agent did not include the use of electricity itself as one of the agencies which Mr. Edison had borrowed as a proof that his lamp would not and could not burn.

It never seems to occur to these invidious electricians that the man who makes a thing go is the man who is entitled to credit, and that the man who makes a failure is entitled to no further credit than for his good intentions and the labor and money he has expended. If the men who make failures are to be entitled to credit, if those who have accomplished nothing are the real geniuses and are allowed to usurp the places of those who have, wherein is the world to be benefited, or how is scientific progress to be advanced? Nothing succeeds in this world like success.

The problem in this case was to produce a practical and economical light by the use of electricity. To accomplish this desirable consummation scientific men have been applying certain agencies in various parts of the world. They have all used the same agencies under the operation of the same natural laws. They have failed; and Mr. Edison, with the same means, has succeeded. They did not make their lamps burn; Mr. Edison did. It is of no consequence that he used the same materials and processes. The thing that the world wanted was the lamp burning. The information that the world wanted was to find out the man who could make the thing go. And it has found it. It knows that the lamp is burning, and that Mr. Edison is the man who has made it go. If he has employed the same agencies as the others, with success, where they made failures, then all the more credit to him, because he is their superior in skill and knowledge. When they can show that his lamp does not burn, it will be time for them to depreciate Mr. Edison; at present they are only declaring their own failures and advertising their own ignorance.

THE "STRONG MAN" CRY

February 28, 1880

Gen. Grant had served two terms as President when he was succeeded by Hayes in 1877. A faction of Republicans sought to nominate the general for a third term in 1880. This editorial, and others published as the convention drew nearer, played a large part in organizing sentiment against a break in the third term tradition.

The cry for "a strong man" is often heard now in the ward-meetings. Candidates for office who think they may ride into power on a wave of popular passion which they have themselves created are fond of saying that the country needs and must have in this emergency "a strong man." How far this demand is based on a cool examination of reasons, and how far on hero-worship and proper admiration for a great figure in our history, it is perhaps impossible to say. But we may at least detect some errors in the common assumption that there is but one "strong" man in the country, and

that the safety of the Republic would be imperiled by the election of anybody else to the Presidency.

There are different kinds of strong men. A man need not have a military education to be strong. The founders of the Republican party were not strong in that sense. Many of them were preachers, and not a few Quakers avowing and practicing the gospel of peace. Abraham Lincoln was a strong man, yet his military experience was confined to a few weeks' service in the Blackhawk War, in which scarcely a gun was fired. Joshua R. Giddings, Charles Sumner, Ben Wade, William Lloyd Garrison, Owen Lovejoy, and a host of others who suffered that the slave might be free, were strong men. The lamented Zachariah Chandler, one of the strongest characters this country ever produced, had the education of a drygoods clerk, not that of a military man.

Nor is it true, again, that among the military men now living there is but one who can be trusted,—but one who would lead the people against a band of usurpers,—but one who would be disposed to see that the Republican party had its rights. William Tecumseh Sherman is a strong man. No doubt can be felt of his firmness, his decision of character, his integrity, his willingness to see that justice is done though the heavens fall. Philip H. Sheridan is another strong man. Nobody ever suspected him of leaning to the side of the Rebel Brigadiers, except with a sabre in his hand. The Republicanism of both of these distinguished Generals is unquestioned. While they would countenance no wrong,

56

they would preserve the right. No Democratic President can be seated by force or fraud while they remain General and Lieutenant-General of the Army of the United States. One blast upon their bugle-horns were worth a million men.

Some men are strong for one purpose and some for the other. War is the natural field of action of one class and peace of another. The qualities which make a man preeminent in one field may partially disqualify him for usefulness in the other. According to the fitness of a man for a special kind of work is his strength or weakness for undertaking that work. The strength of a man in a Republic like ours depends upon his strength with the people; and the latter again depends upon the position to which he aspires, and the circumstances in which the country is placed. A man may be strong in the affections of the people as one who has conferred inestimable services on the Republic, and who has been always modest, dauntless, true; and yet weak with the people as the unwilling candidate of politicians for an office which he has already twice filled.

To be strong as the spontaneous choice of the people is one thing; to be strong by the force of political expedients is quite another thing. To be a strong man with an army at one's back is easy; to be strong by virtue of the united support of a joyful people is still easier. Without the people no man is strong; with them, no man is weak. There is not a Republican candidate for President now before the country who, with 5,000,000 voters at his back, and with the advice of Republican

statesmen and the willing swords of Republican Generals proffered in his behalf, could fail to become President if he should be elected.

The demand for a strong man too often implies belief in a weak people. Strong men have overthrown Republics before now. We do not believe that a strong man could or would impair in the least degree the integrity of our institutions; but we do say it will be a sad day for Republican America if she is ever compelled to confess that one man alone is strong for her, and that without him the perpetuity of her free institutions would be imperiled. The power of 5,000,000 of thinking men is of itself an enormous force; and at least that number could be depended upon to rally to the Republican standard if ever it should be raised in a just cause. It is comparatively a small question who might be the leader of that host. "It would be invincible against any force that the enemy might send."

No strong man elected by the people in November next can legally enter upon the Presidential office until March 4, 1881. The person elected, whoever he may be, will have no more authority over the army of the United States until March 4, 1881, than the meanest civilian now possesses. The strong man the Republican party has to depend upon until that time is Rutherford B. Hayes, of Ohio, President of the United States. As Mr. Hayes could do nothing toward putting himself in in 1877, so Gen. Grant himself, if he should be elected, could now do nothing toward putting himself in. The strongest man the Republican party can have under these circumstances is the one who can command the most votes and obtain a majority so overwhelming that there can be no possibility of a conflict.

The Republican party has claims upon all its strong men, and will have the services of all if any attempt at usurpation is made. There is not among them one so mean and selfish that he would withhold his support if he should not be the first choice of the people for the Presidency. If Mr. Blaine, or Mr. Washburne, or Mr. Edmunds, or Mr. Garfield, or Mr. Windom, or any other man is fairly elected President of the United States, and if his election is disputed, the people will see at the head of the column determined to put him in Gens. Grant, Sherman, and Sheridan, and a host of other distinguished leaders from civil, as well as from military, life. If our cause is strong, we shall be strong; and there is no power on earth that can prevent the Republican party from enjoying the fruits of a victory honestly won whoever may be the candidate for President.

WHAT AMERICA MIGHT DO FOR GREAT BRITAIN

December 28, 1880

A suggestion from England that America carry its share of the white man's burden receives an unexpected reply.

In a recent issue of THE TRIBUNE we reprinted an article from the London *Spectator* setting forth as an English grievance the extraordinary statement that the United States, though exceedingly powerful and rich, "is doing nothing for the world." In the course of this article the *Spectator* said:

"The economic condition of the Union is marvelous, and a just source of pride to its people, but Americans must not forget that much of their brimming prosperity is purchased at a heavy moral price. They do less for the world involving self-sacrifice, deliberately do less, than any great people in it, unless it be the Germans, who may fairly plead that their gigantic armaments, if they produce unrest, still save Europe from the ambition alike of Gaul and Slav.

"The American Union is rich beyond compare, first, because it inherited the richest estate in the world, and secondly, because it spends so little of the National fortune on either army or navy, because it refuses to maintain order in any Asiatic dependency, because it looks on the struggles of the Old World with the half-amused glance of an indifferent spectator. It has the strongest, the freest, and the most prosperous of people within its borders; but no nation in bonds looks upward to the Great Republic for aid, no struggling people turns to her fleet with longing, no perishing race so much as hopes that the Western rifle will drive away the oppressor. One American shell would liberate the Armenians, but it will not be fired. The world may die of despair, for all the Americans care. The most generous individually of races will collectively strike no blow for foreign freedom, send no fleet, issue even no command. We know

58

of no great service she has done to mankind, except in offering the distressed a home—and that repays her.

"Yet, with her necessary disinterestedness, and her magnificent resources, and her detached policy, the Union might often be the best of arbiters, might arrest a war, and hurry on a work of mercy to mankind like the erasure of the Sultanet. She, however, does nothing, even on her own continent, where State after State is rotting down or falling back from civilization, unaided, unguided, and uncontrolled by the mighty people who claim to be distinctively "the Americans," and who endlessly accumulate the strength they use politically only for themselves. The Union does not even insist on order in Mexico, and allows wars to go on in the Southern Continent which she could stop with a word. It will not, we believe, always be so. We do not conceive it possible for so great a State to remain isolated, as if in another planet; but up to to-day America has sought and gained her own happiness by indifference to that of the inhabitants of the remainder of the world."

In other words, because the United States is rich and powerful the *Spectator* would have it pause in its great work of feeding, sheltering, and educating the refugee oppressed of all nations, and start out like another Don Quixote, upon a crusade for the settlement of political questions at issue between nations, to pull down this people and build up that, to get into all sorts of entangling alliances, and to reform everything that needs it. And so confident is the *Spectator* of our abilities in this direction that it believes one shell from an American gun would liberate the oppressed Armenian Christians from the brutal Turk, secure Greece her coveted territory, hurl the Sick Man of Europe from his tottering throne, and pull Chili and Peru apart, thereby saving the value of their bonds which are held in England.

Well, suppose we acted on the *Spectator's* suggestion and became the chief intimidating, intermeddling Power in the world; suppose that by fleets and armies we forced ourselves upon the European Powers, entered into alliances with and against them, engaged in foreign wars of liberation upon the great principle of philanthropy! How would the *Spectator* relish it if the first Power we took in hand to reform were Great Britain herself? For the first impulse of Americans would be to compel her to cease the persecution of weaker peoples.

Our program would probably be something like this: (1) We should say to Great Britain, "Cease your starvation and robbery of the Irish. Give them a chance to live. Cease compelling us to support the victims of your infamous feudal land laws." (2) Stop forcing opium on China, the most brutalizing and debasing of all traffic. (3) We should next drive Great Britain off from American soil and American waters, liberate the Canadas, and hoist the Stars and Stripes upon the Dominion territory, regarding England as an alien who has no business over here. (4) We should probably expel her from off the West Indies, and set independent governments there under our protection. (5) We should seize the Bermudas in retaliation for her having made them the base for blockade-runners, supplying the Rebels with aid and comfort during the War of the Rebellion. (6) Deeming the English navy too strong for international safety and comfort, we should probably enter into an alliance with France and Germany to cut it down to reasonable limits. (7) Having done these things, we should then compel her to do her Christian duty by India, and instantly carry out the promises she made to Greece four years ago; and then commence a compulsory missionary work in England to reform her feudal land laws and redress the grievances of her people at home.

After the British Government had had a sufficient taste of this kind of intermeddling reform, how long would it be before she would think it best for us to stick to our "Washington policy" of "avoiding entangling alliances" with other nations and minding our own business? There is no danger that the United States will ever do otherwise, but we merely throw out these hints to show England what our first great works of international reform would probably be. The Americans are doing well now by minding their own business, and in the future as in the past they are likely to stick to it.

———

THE LEADING AMERICAN JOURNAL

May 16, 1881

A report of progress, in which the slogan, "The World's Greatest News-paper," is all but formulated. The tabulation is of great interest to students of journalism because few such detailed figures of circulation and advertising are available for newspapers of the period.

It is interesting to note that in addition to the long-term rise in circulation, there was also the seasonal increase which publishers at a much later period learned to expect in the late winter and early spring months. The seasonal peak in 1881 seems to have been reached on April 10.

THE CHICAGO TRIBUNE acknowledges no rivalry in business outside of New York. And it is only a question of time when that rivalry shall cease. THE TRIBUNE will be the most successful newspaper on this continent in a pecuniary way as surely as Chicago will outstrip all other cities. As a news-gatherer THE TRIBUNE is already the leading American newspaper. It uses the telegraph more freely and more wisely than any other journal; it has a larger and better staff of correspondents than any other; its news is better edited and more judiciously displayed than that of any of its contemporaries. It does not throw the burden of selection, arrangement, and distribution upon its readers; but gives them *all* the news in condensed and convenient form.

The growth of THE TRIBUNE's business has been unexampled in the history of American journalism. The evidence of this fact is contained in the record of its books during the spring season just drawing to a close. In the last four months and a half it has printed regularly the largest Sunday morning editions ever known in Chicago. Its advertising patronage has been far greater than any enjoyed before in its own experience, and of course more than that of all its local contemporaries combined; and at the same time its size has been increased that its readers have enjoyed a larger amount and variety of reading than ever before.

The following tabulated statement shows the number of pages in each Sunday morning issue since the first of the year, the columns and number of advertisements in each, and the number of papers printed and sold from Jan. 2 to May 15, inclusive:

Date.	Pages	Columns advertisements	Number advertisements	No. of papers printed and sold
Jan. 2	16	27	1,450	53,085
Jan. 9	16	36¼	1,490	52,150
Jan. 16	16	39¾	1,439	54,736
Jan. 23	16	45	1,210	54,202
Jan. 30	18	42½	1,554	59,917
Feb. 6	18	42¼	1,227	59,182
Feb. 13	18	43	1,239	59,213
Feb. 20	18	42½	1,241	60,609
Feb. 27	18	49	1,449	62,235
March 6	18	41	1,274	62,360
March 13	18	48¼	1,360	63,120
March 20	18	40½	1,304	60,065
March 27	20	61	1,887	62,433
April 3	20	65¼	1,964	64,643
April 10	20	73½	2,297	65,079
April 17	24	77	2,637	63,052
April 24	24	88	3,384	62,684
May 1	20	72½	3,081	61,847
May 8	18	63	2,168	62,539
May 15	20	70	2,433	61,138

We defy any newspaper west of New York to present a statement that will match the one given above in any particular. The thing cannot be done. There is no comparison between THE TRIBUNE and its so-called rivals. They are rivals only in their own estimation. To find a real rival to THE TRIBUNE it will be necessary to travel 1,000 miles away, and in all respects except its advertising patronage, which is wonderful for the size of the city which

supports it, THE TRIBUNE has no rival in the world—it is the best newspaper printed.

———

THE ANARCHIST CAN BE LEGALLY PUNISHED

May 6, 1886

Eight policemen were killed and many more were injured in the Haymarket riot of May 4, 1886. The editorial which follows is of considerable interest, pointing as it does toward the legal theory on which the subsequent convictions were obtained. It should be noted, however, that the editor stressses the necessity of proving that the agitators encouraged and advised not murder in general, but this particular murder.

Of the eight defendants in the trial, seven were sentenced to death and the other to 15 years imprisonment. Gov. Oglesby commuted two of the death sentences to life imprisonment. Four of those found guilty were hanged on Nov. 11, 1887 and the fifth killed himself. The other three were pardoned six years later by Gov. Altgeld.

Illinois has no statute precisely like that under which Herr Most was recently indicted in New York for inciting riot by incendiary and in-

JOHANN JOSEPH MOST (1846-1906), a German anarchist, was a member of the reichstag from 1874 to 1878. He edited the *Freie Presse* in Berlin until he was expelled from the Socialist party and moved to France. Ordered out of France, he went to England where he founded *Die Freiheit*. After serving an 18 months sentence there for publishing an article commending the assassins of Alexander II of Russia, he came to America and resumed the publication of his paper. A speech, delivered in 1886, calling upon the workmen of New York to arm themselves for battle led to his conviction and a year's sentence. He was given the same sentence in 1901 for writing approvingly of the assassination of President McKinley. He died in Cincinnati.

flammatory harangues, but the provision of our criminal code in reference to accessories is very broad and will surely cover the case of all such offenders when crime follows their seditious utterances. The sections in question reads:

An accessory is he who stands by and aids, abets, or assists, or who, not being present aiding, abetting, or assisting, hath advised, encouraged, aided, or abetted the perpetration of the crime. He who thus aids, abets, assists, advises, or encourages shall be considered as principal and punished accordingly.

Can it be said that the Anarchist leaders did not "advise or encourage" the bomb-throwing and murder of policemen on Desplaines street? Have they not for years past been advising and encouraging just such crimes? It will be observed that the law applies not only to those on the ground aiding and abetting the act at the time of its commission, but to all not present who had previously "advised, encouraged, aided, or abetted the perpetration of the crime." In all such cases there is no distinction between the principal and the accessory, but the same punishment is provided for both in the following section:

Every such accessory, when a crime is committed within or without this State by his aid or procurement in this State, may be indicted and convicted at the same time as the principal, or before or after his conviction, and whether the principal

is convicted or amenable to justice, or not, and punished as principal.

If it can be shown by clear, direct evidence that the Anarchist leaders "advised and encouraged" the crime perpetrated on Desplaines street they stand in the same position as the bomb-thrower, and under the laws of this State are subject to the punishment of death on the gallows. It remains only to be seen whether they can be shown guilty not simply of encouraging and advising murder in general but of this particular act.

But if evidence cannot be obtained proving direct responsibility for a particular murder, there is surely enough to hold the Anarchist leaders under the Conspiracy law for conspiring "to do an illegal act injurious to police and administration of justice," the penalty for which offense may be fixed at imprisonment in the penitentiary for three years. That they are guilty of this offense is proved by their public threats and overt acts.

Whether they can be punished as accessories to a murder will depend on the proofs found among their papers and documents, which have been already seized by the police, or by facts which may be unearthed in any other manner. But supposing that all such evidence should fail there can be no doubt that the Communistic agitators are guilty of conspiracy at least, and may be imprisoned in the penitentiary for the term prescribed for felons of that class. The law is sufficient for their punishment according to the degree of guilt established by the proofs, and the time has certainly come for it to be rigidly enforced.

―――

THE OPENING OF THE FAIR

May 2, 1893

The Columbian exposition of '93 opens and the editorial writer shoots the rhetorical works. His piece is included in the collection to show young editorial writers—and some older ones —the wisdom of keeping their shirts on, no matter what.

Amid a profound silence, which was far more impressive than would have been the blare of trumpets or the roar of cannon, the Columbian Exposition was opened a few minutes after noon yesterday by a touch from the finger of Grover Cleveland, President of the United States. True, the electric pulsation which by that simple act was sent around the World's Fair, setting in motion its mighty engines, causing the mammoth fountains to flow, and constituting the signal for the unveiling of the typical statue and the unfurling of many hundreds of flags to the breeze, was announced immediately afterwards by the beating of drums and the blowing of steam whistles, this being quickly responded to by a salvo of distant artillery. But it was as if the "still small voice" had been succeeded by the whirlwind, the earthquake, and the fire in which were not the power that afterwards manifested itself in soft tones to the prophet of Israel. Scarcely had these mere noises died away when the band struck up the tune "America," and that produced an electrical effect indeed, for the vast assemblage of people joined in singing the second verse on being invited by Director-General Davis to do so.

That one little movement by President Cleveland actualized more than the wildest day dreams of old time thinkers in all the ages. It called into activity and animated, with the breath of life, a greater mass and variety of organization than was ever supposed to be affected by a fiat from Olympus or controlled by the decrees of Fate to be worked out by the three sisters.

Compare the most important products from the forge of Vulcan with the mammoth engines in Machinery Hall and the mightiest acts the mythologists have ascribed to the "Cloud Compelling" Jupiter with the Titanic forces that keep those engines in motion and which are distributed from them to all parts of the Fair. Contrast the electric incandescence there with the fire fabled to have been brought down from heaven by Prometheus, or its dynamos with the car which the poets sung of as being drawn daily around the ethereal vault by the winged horses of Helios. Measure the products of human brain power and muscular energy there displayed against the reported results of the twelve labors of the far-famed Hercules, the magnificence of the array at Jackson Park with the splendor of the palace built by the genii for Aladdin, and the feasts of the swift-winged messenger of the gods with

GEORGE R. DAVIS (1840-1899) enlisted as a private in the 8th Massachusetts in the Civil war and rose to the rank of colonel. He served in congress from 1879 to 1885 and was treasurer of Cook county from 1886 to 1890.

what was accomplished yesterday by the mere tapping of a telegraph key. The imaginative product of the ages fades into insignificance before the fact of today as a fixed star pales its light in the presence of the midday sun. Nor could the sculptors and painters of classic times around the shores of the Mediterranean avoid turning green with envy if allowed to revisit the pale glimpses of the moon and see the wealth of art production that is grouped on a few acres of land near the head of Lake Michigan.

The Columbian exhibit is also a grandly imposing one, if not equally strong, in comparison with any grouping of modern facts that can be found elsewhere. Far surpassing all previous displays of collection it may be described as an immense epitome of what is prominently valuable in modern progress, and of much that illustrates the historical steps by which that progress has been achieved. It is contributed to by the principal countries of the world. They have joined in projecting into this city as a focus the rays of light which illuminate what were formerly dark places on the face of the earth, and doing so in celebration of the discovery which four centuries ago added another hemisphere to that previously known of by dwellers on the eastern side of the broad Atlantic. The assemblage is one of peoples as well as of material. They have come from far and near to present to those who attend the Columbian gathering what man himself has been defined to be—a microcosm—a miniature condensation as well as representation of the human race in its diverse elements, its present status, and its achievements.

As composed of the most representative men from the different peoples of this and other lands, the concourse of yesterday was the most fitting and appropriate that could have been chosen to inaugurate the great World's Fair. The occasion was not more distinguished by the presence of the President of the United States than he was honored by handling the master key which opened up the Exposition to the public gaze. Participation in any capacity in such a ceremony is something of which the highest dignitary in the land may well be proud, and speak of it in after years to his descendants as one of the most memorable events of his career. It will be especially a red letter day for those who live in Chicago and are intimately identified with its progress from the nothingness of little more than half a century ago to the position of second city in the greatest country of the New World, the discovery of which is celebrated by the holding of the Fair in our midst.

THE PRESIDENT'S WARNING TO ENGLAND

December 18, 1895

The dispute over the British Guiana-Venezuela boundary led to threats of British military action to gain the territory in question. President Cleveland thereupon invoked the Monroe doctrine. The Democratic President is here assured that he will have the support of the Republican congress

64

in any action he may be forced to take.

Britain soon changed her tune and accepted arbitration. In the end, most of her claims were sustained.

The editorial in its original form contained lengthy quotations from President Cleveland's message to congress, which have been omitted here.

The long looked for special message of President Cleveland upon the boundary dispute between Venezuela and Great Britain, and incidentally upon the reply of the Marquis of Salisbury to Secretary Olney, was transmitted to Congress yesterday. It is almost needless to say that it was enthusiastically applauded by the overwhelming majority in the House and that the flaccid, impotent minority sat silent.

The message is a strong, forceful, and clearly stated exposition of the attitude of the government, first, as concerns the Monroe doctrine, and, second, as respects the refusal of the English Government to arbitrate the question in dispute with Venezuela. This being necessitated by the twofold nature of Lord Salisbury's reply.

In his first communication Salisbury takes the extraordinary position that the Monroe doctrine is not applicable "to the state of things in which we live in the present day"; that it is specially inapplicable to a controversy involving the boundary line in question; and, lastly, that it does not embody any principle of international law which is founded on the general consent of nations, and that "no statesman, however eminent, and no nation, however powerful, are competent to insert into the code of international law a novel principle which was never recognized before and which has not since been accepted by the government of any other country."

To each of these claims President Cleveland makes a strong, dignified, and determined reply, the meaning of which is that this country will "stand pat"—that is, that Congress should proceed to enforce the principle of the Monroe doctrine as a matter of vital concern to the people and the safety of the government.

He enters into no detailed argument. He contents himself with declaring that the doctrine was intended to apply to every stage of our national life, and cannot become obsolete.

There is no mistaking the President's attitude on the question of the meaning and of the maintenance of the Monroe doctrine, and there is equally no question that the Republican Congress will sustain him enthusiastically and patriotically.

As to the second communication of the Marquis of Salisbury, in which he declines to arbitrate, the President expresses his disappointment and pointedly criticizes the rejection of an appeal addressed to the magnanimity of a great power in its dealings with a weak and small power. But this being the attitude of Great Britain, we must "accept the situation, recognize the plain requirement, and deal with it accordingly." The way in which the President advises Congress to deal with it is this: Assuming that the contention of Venezuela remains unchanged, Congress should appoint a commission to investigate and determine what is the true boundary

65

line and report as speedily as possible. When such report is made and accepted then the United States should "resist by every means in its power as a willful aggression upon its rights and interests the appropriation by Great Britain of any lands or the exercise of governmental jurisdiction over any territory which, after investigation, we have determined of right belong to Venezuela."

This proposition of the President's involves a question of considerable time. It may be a year before such a commission could make a fair and exhaustive report. Meanwhile if Venezuela of her own motion as the result of negotiations with Great Britain should come to an agreement the work of the commission would be superfluous, as objection cannot be made to what she does of her own free will. But on the other hand the position of Venezuela will be strengthened by the President's message and she will now feel that the power of the United States is behind her and that the Monroe doctrine applies in her case or will be made to apply. In any event it is questionable whether under the Monroe doctrine South American republics can give away their territory to foreign nations.

However the boundary dispute may eventuate, the thanks of the country are due to President Cleveland for his vigorous, resolute, fearless, and patriotic defense of that doctrine. In this respect he has risen to the necessities of the situation and left no doubt in the minds of European politicians where this government stands on the question of the Monroe doctrine. They are notified that so far from being obsolete, it is a live, practical doctrine and England is notified it applies to this boundary dispute. There need be no fear that this Republican Congress will not stand by the President in his patriotic American attitude. If Great Britain refuses to accept the Monroe doctrine "let her bring on her bears." She will find Uncle Sam ready to receive them.

IS THE "COMMERCIAL SPIRIT" TO RULE?

March 2, 1898

Feb. 15, 1898. Following an explosion, the U.S.S. Maine sank in the harbor of Havana, Cuba, with the loss of 266 lives.

March 20. A naval board of inquiry attributed the loss of the ship to an exterior mine.

April 20. President McKinley approved a congressional resolution demanding that Spain withdraw from Cuba, and required a reply from Spain by April 23.

April 24. Spain declared war.

April 25. Congress declared that war with Spain had begun three days before.

The Washington dispatches printed in yesterday's TRIBUNE stated that—

In the absence of exciting news from Havana and the transfer of the court of inquiry to Key West there has been a noticeable cessation of the war talk here in Washington. The conservative attitude of the President has been reflected in Congress, and members who last week would listen to nothing but war are now disposed to wait patiently for the actual decision by the court of inquiry.

66

When is that decision to be made public? The court of inquiry is now at Key West. From there it is to return to Havana and await whatever reports may be made by the divers who are slowly investigating the condition of the wrecked warship.

Is that court making all the haste it can to get through so that its conclusions may be laid before the public, or have its members received a quiet tip from the Navy Department or from some other quarter to the effect that they must make haste slowly and continue searching for evidence long after they may have all the evidence they need to fix the guilt of the destruction of the Maine on the Spaniards?

If the court has been advised to procrastinate, the question whether that advice should be praised or condemned would depend on the motive that prompted it. If President McKinley, though convinced that the Spaniards were guilty and that war was inevitable, should feel that necessary preparation remained to be made, procrastination would be proper. The people would indorse his action.

But if the court of inquiry has received an intimation that delay will be acceptable, is the motive back of that advice commendable? Or is delay desired in order that the public may cool down and the "war talk" die away? Is time to be gained to enable the Tories and the cowards—mugwumps and jack rabbits— to drug into slumber the patriotic impulses and the just resentment of the people? Are they to be given time in which to use their hypodermic syringes and inject morphine into the

veins of the body politic?

Has the administration fallen under the baleful influence of the unpatriotic Americans? Is it intended that when the report of the court of inquiry has been received it shall be wrapped up in stout paper, tied up with much red tape, sealed with many seals, and tucked away in the remote pigeon hole where dust may accumulate on it during the coming years?

Is it intended, when the first flush of indignation over the treacherous murder of American seamen has abated, to suggest to bankrupt Spain that if it will hand over some pesetas or some of its shinplasters nothing more will be said about the Maine and it may go on murdering Cubans to its heart's content?

Great activity is being displayed at every navy yard and arsenal. Ships which were laid up are being prepared for service. Guns are being mounted. The ordnance factories are running night and day. Are these serious preparations or are they a sham, designed to amuse and deceive the people?

When all the work now in hand is finished are the people to be told that they must wait a little longer— that further preparations must be made? Are the people to be told that Chicago and the other lake ports must be fortified so that they may not be exposed to attack by a Spanish fleet?

The preparations which are making now ought to be made. But do they mean anything? Will swift action follow on the heels of their completion? Or will one delay follow another until the patriotic ardor of

Americans has cooled down? THE TRIBUNE does not think so.

That commercial spirit which believes that speculation is the chief end of man is gaining strength in this country. It is laboring to poison patriotism at the fountain. It seeks to make Americans believe that dishonor, shame, humiliation should be submitted to cheerfully sooner than that the stock market should be disturbed or the revelries of the "400" be interfered with.

That base commercial spirit, acting in unison with the mugwumpery of the country, is trying to gain admission to the councils of the nation and to hypnotize Congress and the President so that they may do its cowardly will. Is the commercial spirit to rule, the country to be disgraced, and the name of McKinley to be bracketed with that of Buchanan?

Or is the unpardonable insult which this country has received to be atoned for by the expulsion of the Spaniards from Cuba? Patriotic Americans hope for the latter. They believe the administration feels as they do.

———

TRUSTS SOWING THE WIND

April 20, 1899

In Europe, business combinations in restraint of trade have generally been lawful. In America, public opinion forced congress to outlaw the so-called trusts. The Sherman act was passed in 1890, nine years before this editorial appeared. Enforcement at first was not vigorous, however, and it was not until many editorials such as this one focused attention on monopolistic abuses that important prosecutions were instituted. A few years later, in the Presidency of Theodore Roosevelt, suits were begun against the tobacco combination and Standard Oil, among others of the sort. The orders dissolving the two combinations were affirmed by the Supreme court in 1911.

The Republicans did include an anti-trust plank in their 1900 platform, as they were urged to do here. It became the charter for Mr. Roosevelt's subsequent activities directed against monopolies.

The tobacco trust has absorbed a large St. Louis tobacco factory, the control of which it has long been anxious to get. Mr. Wetmore, one of the stockholders in the factory, fought consolidation, but in vain. Being defeated, he had to sell his stock and give up his position. Day before yesterday he called the 3,000 factory employes into the street and made them a farewell address. His closing words, which brought out enthusiastic cheers, were:

"With the control in my own hands I never, never would have consented to the sale of this plant to a trust. But I was only one man against a mighty corporation, and my powers of persuasion at last failed. Still, I think the fight will yet be won, and I propose to remain in it to the finish. I expect to devote all my time, all my energies, and all my wealth to aid in the fight against these giant combinations that are fast ruining the business of the country."

The Republican or Democratic politician who sees in this occurrence at St. Louis merely an angry man venting his wrath against those who have "frozen him out," makes a serious mistake. What has happened at St. Louis is happening elsewhere, only on a far more extensive scale. The St. Louis case differs from others only in that the victim dared to speak out. There have been many other instances where the freezing out process has been applied not to one man, as in this case, but to hundreds of men.

Often during the last few years a trust has deemed it necessary to get control of a factory in some small town in order to get rid of its possible competition. Having obtained control, the trust closes the factory because it can make more cheaply elsewhere all the products it intends to market. It happens frequently that that small factory is the mainstay of a little town. Its citizens may have paid out money to secure its establishment. Its employes are the best customers of the local stores. When the plant is idle and the workmen have to leave to get employment elsewhere the town decays. There are now in Ohio and many other Northern States "deserted villages" which are desolate because trusts have killed off the industries which throve there once.

Mr. Wetmore has lost his position, but he has some money to fall back on. He is fortunate, for of the men of his age whom the trusts throw out of their positions few have any money or are able to find anything else to do. The lot of a man over 40 who is "trusted" out of the place he has been holding is pathetically hard. He seeks for work. His field of search is limited, for he has been trained to do only one thing. He finds nothing to do in that limited field, for wherever he goes he finds he is "too old." The preference is given to "young men." If there is a place vacant such as he used to fill he is told that it is deemed best to give it to one of the young men working for the firm who entered its service as a boy. He is told the firm believes in the merit system.

There are thousands of middle-aged men in this country who resent the wrongs the trusts have done them as keenly as Mr. Wetmore does. There are tens of thousands of working men who have been thrown out of work by the trusts. There are villages and towns whose industries have been blighted by the trusts.

The managers of the two great parties may prepare themselves to be asked searching questions soon. The Democratic managers will be asked to explain why so many of their leading men have been closely associated with great trusts. Senator Brice was, while alive. William C. Whitney is now. It is said in the yellow newspapers that he has made a hundred million in a few years out of local and general monopolies.

The Republican managers will be asked if their party, whose platform denounced trusts in 1892, but was silent in 1896, means to be equally silent in 1900. They will be asked whether they agree with Senator Lodge in his statement that a dec-

CALVIN STEWART BRICE (1845-1898) was United States senator from Ohio from 1891 to 1897. He was a railroad president and a director of a long list of companies including the Chase National Bank of New York.

WILLIAM C. WHITNEY (1841-1904) was President Cleveland's distinguished secretary of the navy. He was a man of great wealth. As a Wall street lawyer and financier he was active in the organization of a number of public utility companies.

HENRY CABOT LODGE (1850-1924) served as United States senator from Massachusetts from 1893 until his death.

69

laration against trusts will be "buncombe." Are they prepared to assert that trusts, when protected by tariffs or railroad discriminations, are as innocent as trusts which have no artificial advantages and live or die on their merits?

The Republican party must prepare to meet a new issue. The silver question is being thrust into the background. The war issue is dead. Peace has been made with Spain and the war now going on in the Philippines is not bringing in much glory. The trusts are to be the issue of 1900. Both parties will have to recognize that fact soon. The Republican party should recognize it first.

THE PASSING OF THE CENTURY

January 1, 1901

If the twentieth century is to live up to the high hopes for it expressed here, it had better get started. Otherwise this editorial, and particularly the last paragraph, must stand as a masterpiece of wishful thinking and false prophecy.

Exit the nineteenth, enter the twentieth century. In the flight of the years centuries count for little, but they mark time as the procession of the years goes by. Considering the millions of years that must have elapsed since primitive man appeared, and the millions more that must have passed before his coming, and the 3,300,000 more, if Professor See be correct, that will pass before the dead sun gives out no more heat and light and humanity

disappears, a century is but an infinitesimal point, but it is useful for making comparative measurements and fixing dates in the world's progress.

Comparatively brief as the time has been, the accomplishments of the nineteenth century have been astonishing. In the development of commerce, the growth of population, the discoveries in industry, the expansion of energy and prosperity, the lifting of economic burdens, the growth of knowledge, the improvement of methods that make life easier and safer, and in moral, educational, and religious conquest the century's achievements almost bewilder conception. It has been preeminently the century of usefulness. It has given the world the telegraph, telephone, ocean cable, sewing machine, electric light, trolleys, harvesting machines, railroads, the first practical steamboats, anaesthetics, postage stamps, envelopes, cooking stoves, and other articles of common use, besides preparing the way for future uses of the powers of nature which will be developed in the twentieth century.

It has not surpassed its predecessors, however, in the development of beauty or in the progress of art, architecture, music, or literature. No architect can be named greater than he who wrought the Parthenon. No sculptor has caught the majesty of Michael Angelo or Phidias, no painter the beauty of Apelles or Raphael. No musician has rivaled

THOMAS J. J. SEE was professor of astronomy at the University of Chicago from 1893 to 1896 and at the time this editorial appeared was a professor of mathematics in the Navy. He now lives in California.

70

the harmonies or skill of Sebastian Bach. Homer, Eschylus, Shakespeare, and Dante still dwell upon heights inaccessible to the modern poets and dramatists.

Perhaps the change will come in the twentieth century. The purely material may claim less attention and Mammon come to be less regarded. The commercial spirit, always destructive to art, may give place to a renaissance of art in its varied forms, and in the new cycle even greater apostles of beauty may appear. The world may have less of the useful and more of the beautiful. The intellect of mankind, tiring of the material, may turn towards the higher things, and with the advantages of increased education and deeper knowledge of science and nature become notable for grand and diversified achievements.

With the marvelous material progress of the century has come a long train of blessings. The nineteenth century has witnessed a decrease of bigotry, superstition, and ignorance and the abolition of slavery and serfdom. The man never counted for so much in the history of the world as now. The century has witnessed an increase of liberty, free thought, education, religion, progress towards a more perfect manhood, comforts for the many, religious toleration and philanthropy. It has witnessed a vast improvement in appliances for making life more enjoyable and in prolonging it by improved sanitation and greater medical and surgical skill. Pestilences have been almost banished from civilized countries.

The century has witnessed the growth of public sentiment towards reform in social and political spheres of activity and of a sympathy with the poor and oppressed which has busied the most alert minds with plans for alleviating their condition. Standing upon the threshold of the twentieth century it looks as if it would be the century of humanity and a keener realization of the brotherhood of man. This will be a grander achievement than the discoveries of science or the triumphs of art.

THE MINERS' STRIKE
September 7, 1902

The myth that the newspapers of America persistently opposed the rise of trade unionism finds no support in this editorial.

The great anthracite strike, led by John Mitchell, had begun in May, 1902 and was to last until the following March 18. Something like 150,000 miners walked out to obtain higher wages, shorter hours, and recognition of their union. The operators would concede nothing until President Theodore Roosevelt threatened to seize the mines and operate them. In the arbitration which followed, the miners won a 10 percent increase in wages and other concessions.

An approach to general unanimity on the part of the press concerning an economic or social question is so unusual as to deserve attention when it occurs. There is such unanimity in the attitude of the press concerning the anthracite mine owners. There is a general agreement that they have not been so conciliatory towards their employes or so regardful of the public welfare as they might have been. To all who have sought to bring about peace between them and their employes they have cried out "hands off." They have declared bluntly that the mines are their property, and that they have an unlimited, uncontrolled right to do as they please with their own. They refuse to recognize their just obligation either to their employes or to the public.

Property owners have rights. They have, theoretically, a right to employ whom they choose at such wages as they please and to establish such lawful regulations as they see fit with reference to the mode of payment or to the terms of employment. But in society as now organized, there is an obvious connection between the interests of employer and employe. There is also a growing tendency to recognize the obligations of property to the community at large and to labor. The theory that the owner of property has absolute control of it has of late been modified, if not abandoned.

Labor wars have been waged in defense of that theory, and seemingly have been won by the property owners—the employers—but at a fearful cost.

It is unnecessary to recall other strikes than the one of the engineers of the Burlington road, of the Carnegie employes, and of the Pullman men. In each instance the employers won a victory, but they paid a heavy price for it not only in money but in the morale of their service. Looking

THE BURLINGTON strike came in 1888; the Carnegie (Homestead) strike in 1892; and the Pullman strike in 1894.

at the matter from a broader point of view than the monetary interests of the employer, in each instance the contest was distinctly injurious to the community in general. Large numbers of workingmen were embittered against capital. They felt that the Carnegie and Pullman methods were oppressive and tyrannical. In the Pullman case, as in so many other cases, the shibboleth of the employer was "nothing to arbitrate." Arbitration was not conceded, and the Pullman men had to submit. They were resentful. So were the men in other fields of labor who sympathized with them and with the Carnegie and the Burlington strikers. There is not the same feeling of loyalty or attachment to the employer that there formerly was. Perhaps that is to be expected as the number of men working for one employer increases, but at any rate workingmen occupy a position of antagonism to capital and to general employers of labor they did not fifteen or twenty years ago.

It cannot be said the employer has no obligations to the community at large, when he can influence the peace and wellbeing of the community so profoundly by his method of dealing with labor. The strike which is defeated by resorting to harsh and oppressive measures leaves a sting behind it. The public at large may feel the effects of the unjust and unfeeling policy of an employer long after it has ceased to operate.

It would have been for the interests of the people of the United States in general, and the mineowners and mineworkers in particular, if the mineowners had been

72

more conciliatory in their methods or had shown the least willingness to admit that the miners have rights. The men in the mines are entitled not merely to fair wages but to good wages. They have a right to demand that the method of paying them for their work shall be such that they know they are not being cheated. They complain that they mine more coal than they are paid for. That is a grievance which, if well founded, calls for redress. They ask for shorter hours of work. They are not alone in that. For a century workingmen everywhere have been asking for shorter hours.

These are questions which in the opinion of the general public are proper questions for arbitration. The miners may be asking too much. Let the arbitrators pass on the question. When the mineowners say "there is nothing to arbitrate" the answer of the public is that they are in error. They are assuming a position which is untenable nowadays when it is recognized that a business like the one they carry on is affected by a public trust. Property has rights, but it has duties also, and the public, which must protect the rights, will manage in some way to enforce the duties.

The mineowners say they will not "recognize the union." Time was when all employers said that. Few say it now. The leaders of one great industry after another have submitted cheerfully or reluctantly to deal with "an organization." It is admitted by most employers, and by all non-employers, that labor has a right to organize. It has the same right to organize that capital has. The right to recognition follows on the heels of the right to organize.

Sooner or later the mineowners will have to recognize a union. Their speedy acquiescence in the inevitable will save them odium and the public loss.

The mineowners are striving with dull obstinacy against moral forces and tendencies infinitely more powerful than they are. They are the Bourbons, the Tories of the industrial world, the last advocates of the "divine right" of the employer to rule his employes, and of the owner of property to use, misuse, or abuse it as he sees fit without recognition of any obligation to the community.

THE TRIBUNE POLL ON RECIPROCITY

June 3, 1911

Close economic and diplomatic relations with Canada have long been an article of THE TRIBUNE's *creed.*

President Taft succeeded in winning congressional approval of the reciprocal trade agreement he negotiated with Canada, but the program was defeated in the Dominion parliament in 1911.

Elsewhere in this issue of THE TRIBUNE is published the result of a poll of newspapers of the west, daily and weekly—and without regard to political affiliation—on the question of the Canadian reciprocity agreement. Twenty-two states were covered, including the territory most in doubt.

The verdict confirms the belief that President Taft has the support of the country in this policy of broad statesmanship, and THE TRIB-

73

UNE is pleased to be able to make a definite statement of facts at a time when the President comes to Chicago to explain his views on the treaty which he has been successful in submitting to congress.

He has been confident that the central and western states would support this principle, and with a fine courage he has been willing to accept responsibility if they did not. He will be in a better position now to understand that he is speaking to a friendly audience rather than to one which doubts or requires more proofs.

The newspaper editors whose opinions are represented in the poll are safe guides to the sentiment in their communities, and the fact that weekly journals form nearly 90 per cent of the newspapers polled indicates that the opinion of the agricultural districts is voiced.

It may be recalled that when THE TRIBUNE presented the results of a poll showing the feeling of the country towards the conduct of the national house of representatives by Joseph G. Cannon, then speaker, there were scoffers. The short time intervening between the publication of that verdict against "Cannonism" and the revolt of the house itself against his dominance was all that was allowed for the enjoyment of the fallacy that the poll did not represent public opinion.

That poll is accepted now as truly expressive of sentiments which later were fully revealed. The present poll is equally a reliable expression of opinion in the states it covers.

President Taft is in Chicago today. In welcoming him it is a pleasure to assure him that the country supports him as against the conservatives of the Republican party who oppose his policies.

TRUTH WINS; JUSTICE IS DONE

July 15, 1912

The unseating of William Lorimer, Republican senator from Illinois, was a triumph for THE TRIBUNE *which had exposed the bribery of the legislature which elected him.*

The United States senate has given its judgment that the election of William Lorimer by the Illinois legislature May 26, 1909, was brought about by corrupt practices, was tainted, and is void.

The seat occupied by Mr. Lorimer is declared vacant. There was no valid, legal election of a successor to Albert J. Hopkins, whose term expired March 4, 1909.

That brings the Lorimer case to an end so far as the issue was the right of a man to hold a position to which he was elected as the result of bribery. In other respects the general questions involved in the long struggle continue to demand attention. When the thing that had grown at Springfield came to the surface far enough to attract attention, and when an attempt was made to pull it up, it was found that the roots ran in all directions, great, powerful roots extending under business, and the courts, and homes. To uproot them has disordered entire communities.

A great deal has been done. A

74

great deal remains to be done.

So far as Mr. Lorimer is concerned, he is no longer United States senator. He was not expelled. He was not in the controversy except as he projected himself into it. His election, which was assailed, is declared invalid.

A corruption fund was used in connection with the election. It was distributed to men who had voted for Lorimer by men who desired his election. There never was any doubt of this. The confessions of the men who had received the money could not be shouted down, could not be explained, and could not be disproved.

In the period of more than two years in which this case was in the criminal courts and before the Illinois senate and the United States senate, every artifice that shrewd men could devise and money command, whether legitimate or dishonorable, was employed by the interests attacked, and yet the force and effect of the confessions merely grew. Subtleties were of no avail. In its essentials it was a very simple case and could not be disguised.

THE TRIBUNE, which presented the first disclosures by publishing the narrative of Charles A. White, April 30, 1910, did not need the justification of the senate vote which declares the seat vacant. No justification was needed for publishing the truth and insisting upon it, insisting upon it, in spite of discouragement and in spite of malice.

The public knows little of the

CHARLES A. WHITE of O'Fallon was a Democratic member of the Illinois house of representatives whose confession that he had been bribed to vote for Lorimer was a TRIBUNE scoop.

methods adopted by the defense in efforts to stop not only THE TRIBUNE but other newspapers, public officials, and citizens from doing their duty in the matter. The inquiry now being conducted by the Cook county grand jury affords the best insight into these attempts.

It is the belief of THE TRIBUNE that the whole miserable story will come out some day, and that before very long. The crimes committed to protect the men responsible for the crime of May 26, 1909, have been as low and despicable as the original crime itself. Some of them have revealed a far lower morality than that of the briber and bribe taker.

A great deal of good already has come out of this fight against organized corruption. Citizens who have been patient to follow as complications were unraveled and as men were dragged out from shadows are better equipped to understand the relations of corrupt politics and corrupt business. When the secrets were opened up the stench offended and disgusted many people, including some respectable people who wished for the sake of their own peace of mind they might have been spared the knowledge. THE TRIBUNE was conscious all the time that citizens whose respect is worth having were uneasy and at times even resentful. Such feelings, we think, have disappeared.

The snake of corruption in the Illinois legislature has been scotched. It has not been killed, but it has been injured. The legislature is a better body than it was, and it does better work. If it had not been challenged it would have grown in viciousness.

75

The case undoubtedly succeeded in stimulating public conscience all over the nation and making public sensitiveness greater on questions involving honor and honesty. It also did a great deal to hasten the acceptance by the United States senate of the principle of the direct election of senators.

The long struggle would have been worth while even had the election of Lorimer been permitted to stand as valid. If the senate had voted the second time as it voted the first, to sustain the validity of the election, the struggle would have been worth while.

The law has not been able to punish the men whose guilt was apparent, but they have not escaped punishment. They went free from courtrooms and they avoided the penitentiary, but the story is one of broken men. They evaded the law, but they could not avoid retribution. Some have suffered. Others will suffer.

CLARENCE S. FUNK, general manager of the International Harvester Co., informed the senate committee that Edward Hines, the lumberman, approached him a few days after Lorimer's election to solicit a contribution of $10,000 to a fund of $100,000 being raised to cover the costs of buying the senatorship. On Oct. 14, 1911, Funk was sued for $25,000 by a certain John C. Henning who alleged alienation of his wife's affections. Later, Henning and his wife confessed that they had been paid handsomely to start a suit whose purpose was to blacken Funk's reputation. Their witnesses also confessed. The alienation suit was tried in June, 1912. The jury deliberated only 12 minutes before bringing in a verdict for Funk. Daniel Donahoe, Henning's lawyer, was convicted and fined $2,000. He was disbarred in 1917 for his part in the conspiracy and never revealed where the considerable sums given the Hennings and their witnesses came from.
WILLIAM M. BURGESS, called as a witness before the senate committee, testified that on March 8, 1911, C. F. Wiehe, a relative and business associate of Mr. Hines, had boasted of making a contribution of $10,000 to a Lorimer corruption fund. The conversation, Burgess said, took place in the smoking room of a Pullman car.

The manner in which the newspapers of Chicago, of Illinois, and of the nation, with certain easily explained exceptions, took up the cause of decency in government was a heartening thing. It is not for THE TRIBUNE to thank these newspapers. It is allowed merely to note what their activities were and to add its praise to the praises of their readers.

Such citizens as Clarence S. Funk and William Burgess of Duluth, at what hazards the persecution of Mr. Funk shows, dared to do their part courageously and well; and in the United States senate such senators as Kern, Kenyon, Lea, Smith of Michigan, La Follette, Cummins, Borah, Crawford, Works, Root, and others, and in the first investigation Beveridge of Indiana and Frazier of Tennessee, then members, stood squarely for honesty, are entitled to the country's respect for their loyalty to good government, and have helped to strengthen national confidence in congress.

The case was dragged through sewers by the defense, but it has exposed political corruption in its real infamy. It has done good. More would have been done if the men who furnished the money to bribe the legislature and the men who handled it could have been exposed and brought into court.

The record is not yet complete, but the results are salutary.

———

VICTORIOUS DEFEAT

November 6, 1912

The editorial was written when the returns from the Presidential election

76

of 1912 were still incomplete. Wood-row Wilson received 435 electoral votes to 88 for Roosevelt and 8 for Taft; in popular vote Wilson, with 6,286,000, ran more than 2,000,000 ahead of Roosevelt who, in turn, led Taft by better than 650,000.

The Progressives are triumphant in defeat. Theodore Roosevelt is not to be our next president, but considering what he had to overcome he has achieved something like a political miracle. The great vote rolled up by his party is at once a noble tribute to him and an assurance that Progressivism is in the flood and will yet carry the day.

To have brought forth a new party and developed this strength in a three months' campaign is the most remarkable feat in our political history. It could not have been accomplished even under the leadership of Theodore Roosevelt if the cause were not ripe, if the forces for political progress had not been running deeply in the nation's life, if the people had not been ready for forward leadership.

This they have been given inspiringly by Theodore Roosevelt and his supporters. The Progressives have thrown open the doors of a more spacious period than that through which we have passed. They have challenged the best in the American people. They have restored democratic idealism to politics. They have brought into the arena of definite public discussion the pressing problems which the older parties have not dared to deal with save in glittering generalities. They have exposed the superficiality, insincerity, and conventionality of the older

parties' programs, and while keeping their feet upon the solid ground of the most serious actualities have raised political discussion to a higher level.

The remarkable, if not complete and immediate, success of the Progressive campaign has broken the back of bossism. It has repudiated the methods practiced by the Barnes-Penrose-Crane type of political captains, and laid the foundation of a system of real leadership. The "invisible government" exposed in the defense of Lorimerism, exposed again in the Archbold correspondence, exposed again in the fatally successful conspiracy at Chicago to rob the rank and file of the Republican party of their chosen leader—this "invisible government" has received at the hands of Progressive voters the heaviest blow it has yet suffered. It is tottering to its fall. That such strength as the Progressives have shown could be developed in the briefest of political conflicts means that in a few years there will be but one government in these United States, and that visible to the people and responsible to them.

All honor to Theodore Roosevelt and to the men and women who have fought the Progressive fight with him. They have succeeded in

THE ARCHBOLD LETTERS: John D. Archbold, an important official of the Standard Oil company, wrote numerous letters to leading political figures, most of them Republicans in the senate and house. The letters, revealing Archbold's hold over these men and substantial transfers of money to them, were turned over to W. R. Hearst, the publisher, by a couple of Archbold's employes who were paid more than $20,000 for betraying his confidence. The letters, after being photographed, were returned to the oil company's files and it was only in September, 1908, several years afterward, that Mr. Hearst made them public in the course of a political campaign in which he was then engaged.

the highest sense, if not the fullest, and they have done a great constructive service which the future will build upon to their honor and the welfare of the American people.

OUT OF THE DARK

September 11, 1913

The "How to Keep Well" column was a TRIBUNE *innovation in Sept., 1911. It was placed in charge of Dr. W. A. Evans, who had distinguished himself as Chicago's commissioner of health.*

THE TRIBUNE has received a long letter from one of its readers who objects to the plain speaking as well as other features of "How to Keep Well." It is an interesting production, this letter, not because the judgments it expresses are novel or original, but for the opposite reason —because they represent a state of mind, an attitude toward life as old perhaps as the race.

We do not refer to the evidences of personal envy and bias, although they, too, began at the beginning, but to the attitude illustrated in objections to references to venereal disease. If men are not still monkeys it is because man has combated this attitude in the main and got the better of it. Man ceased to be ape when he walked erect, when he held up his head and looked at the world with a level glance, when he ceased to scream and scurry away.

But in all man's struggle upward from the brute there has been the tug back of the coward instinct— "If it is evil don't look, don't grapple

with it, turn your back and run, and if you can't run, shut your eyes and bury your head." Counsel of the banderlog, wisdom of the ostrich.

At the recent international congress of physicians and surgeons in London, the greatest assembly of its kind ever held, one of the most important discussions was that dealing with venereal diseases, an evil which, as one speaker said, comes after tuberculosis and alcoholic abuse as a scourge of mankind. Columns were given the discussion in the London Times and a royal commission has been created to consider measures of correction.

Every one but the ostrich minded is realizing that the folly of ignorance, the conspiracy of silence, must be ended. It has cost too much, it is costing too much. THE TRIBUNE intends to help in lifting this curse, and is no believer in darkness as a cure for anything.

THE TWILIGHT OF THE KINGS

August 2, 1914

This editorial found its way into a thousand scrapbooks. In all probability, it was more widely reprinted than any ever published in THE TRIBUNE. *In glowing words, it exactly expressed the mood of the American people at the beginning of the first world war.*

Twilight was, indeed, descending on the kings. In a few years, the Romanoffs, then the Hapsburgs and Hohenzollerns and half a dozen lesser royalties were to be dethroned; but twilight was descending, also, on the 19th century's easy optimism. The ex-

pectation that tyranny would disappear with the tyrants had soon to be abandoned.

Before establishing hell on earth the pietistic kings commend their subjects to God. Seek the Lord's sanction for the devil's work.

"And now I commend you to God," said the kaiser from his balcony to the people in the street. "Go to church and kneel before God and pray for His help for your gallant army."

Pray that a farmer dragged from a Saxon field shall be speedier with a bayonet thrust than a winemaker taken from his vines in the Aube; that a Berlin lawyer shall be steadier with a rifle than a Moscow merchant; that a machine gun manned by Heidelberg students shall not jam and that one worked by Paris carpenters shall.

Pray that a Bavarian hop grower, armed in a quarrel in which he has no heat, shall outmarch a wheat grower from Poltava; that Cossacks from the Don shall be lured into barbed wire entanglements and caught by masked guns; that an innkeeper of Salzburg shall blow the head off a baker from the Loire.

"Go to church and pray for help" —that the hell shall be hotter in innocent Ardennes than it is in equally innocent Hessen; that it shall be hotter in innocent Kovno than in equally innocent Posen.

And the pietistic czar commends his subjects to God that they may have strength of arm in a quarrel they do not understand; that they may inflict more sufferings than they are required to endure and the name of Romanoff be greater than the name of Hohenzollern, that it may be greater than the name of Hapsburg, that its territories shall be wider and the territories of Hohenzollern and the territories of Hapsburg less.

The pietistic emperor of Austria commends his subjects to God, to seek divine assistance to crush the peasants of Serbia, dragged from the wheat field when it was ready for the scythe and given to the scythe themselves.

This is, we think, the last call of monarchy upon divinity when Asmodeus walks in armor. The kings worship Baal and call it God, but out of the sacrifice will come, we think, a resolution firmly taken to have no more wheat growers and growers of corn, makers of wine, miners and fishers, artisans and traders, sailors and storekeepers offered up with prayer to the Almighty in a feudal slaughter, armed against each other without hate and without cause they know, or, if they know, would not give a penny which way it was determined.

This is the twilight of the kings. Western Europe of the people may be caught in this debacle, but never again. Eastern Europe of the kings will be remade and the name of God shall not give grace to a hundred square miles of broken bodies.

If Divinity enters here it comes with a sword to deliver the people from the sword.

It is the twilight of the kings. The republic marches east in Europe.

IF WE FIGHT GERMANY

June 5, 1915

The Lusitania, a British liner, was sunk by the German submarine, U-20, off southern Ireland on May 7, 1915. Of the 1,198 lives lost, 128 were American. The propagandists for intervention immediately cried for a war of revenge and a war for the defense of international law. A month later, the editor finds no popular demand for the first and little sense in the second. He offers a formula by which Americans may determine whether participation in the war is necessary.

Count von Bernstorff's efforts to preserve peace for this country in its relations with Germany deserve recognition. The German ambassador, although embarrassed by the interruption in his means of communicating with his government, is extraordinarily active in his endeavor to present to Berlin an accurate representation not only of American demands but of the national sentiment behind the demands.

The most apparent error in Germany's policy throughout the war is that it has considered only the ponderables. In a world of sentiment it has endeavored to create a world of fact, evidently not understanding that when the emotions are sitting as judges facts make poor witnesses. Part of the German fury may be explained by saying that the Germans see facts too large and are enraged that the rest of the world does not see them at all or sees them too small.

The elaborate endeavors to prove that the Lusitania carried guns and the insistence upon the fact that it carried ammunition get nowhere against the American sentiment that the killing of noncombatants, women, and children is murder without excuse.

So long as the Germans decline to see the noncombatants on the decks and the Americans decline to see the ammunition in the hold the opening for deadly consequences is wide. Count von Bernstorff is trying with all his power to bring his government to understand that the American position is one which the American sentiment made it obligatory for the government to take. We must try to see the German side.

The loss of life on the Lusitania is irreparable, if not inexpiable. For material damage done American property Germany offers to make recompense. For the safety of American citizens on the sea hereafter it would be possible, with concessions on the part of both the German and American governments, to provide.

We do not believe there is a bit of sentiment in America for a war with Germany merely to punish that nation for the sinking of the Lusitania. However outraged this country was by the destruction of the vessel, there has been no dominating cry from men proclaiming that they would go into the trenches in Flanders to avenge their countrymen. And we do not think there ought to be such a cry. Wars undertaken by a democracy must have or ought to have other cause than one of emotions outraged by a catastrophe, however tragic.

War, in the faulty human scheme of things, can be justified only as the instrument by which a nation works towards its destiny or averts its fate. This excuse is conceded only by nationalists, who, praise be, so long as the human scheme of things remains so immeasurably away from perfection, remain in the majority.

War then, if Americans are to think of it as impending, ought to be considered in the light of our national interest and national egotism. We reject the idea of a peaceful and commercial war as humiliating and abasing. If we fight it must be with human sacrifice and in human suffering. Save us from the obloquy of a tradesman's war when other nations, conscious of their peril or of their rights, are offering their best and strongest.

Is sacrifice to be demanded of us to uphold a matter of international law when to the knowledge of any man the law is upon the point of being changed to follow the course of invention in the instruments of making war?

If we fight let there first be the firm conviction that the wonderful German organization of society, with its military socialism and its indomitable purpose, threatens our loose democracy and its emphasis of the individual, his will, worth, and happiness. Let us be convinced that the overthrow of the nations opposed to Germany would mean the release upon us of the terrific powers of this central European military empire, young and strong and determined.

If we go to war let it be because we see an embodied and threatening menace to our form of life, and not because in the development of the submarine and the wireless and in the new importance of the ammunition factory international law finds itself out of touch with events and impotent to do justice.

Certainly we can find a working adjustment of disputed questions to bridge us over the time of stress. If we go to the final arbitrament let it be with the consciousness that we are working out our national destiny and working for our right to live as we wish to live.

LACK OF AIRCRAFT

August 30, 1915

An early chapter in the organization of the army and navy air forces. This is one among scores of editorials published at this period, calling attention to the nation's lack of adequate military preparation.

The Aero Club of America has been organized to supply the army and navy with aeroplanes, first by encouraging voluntary subscriptions and later by urging legislative action. If successful the club will be in a position to furnish the government with an air service, which in modern warfare is an eye of the army.

Air reconnaissance is no longer an experiment, and an army and navy without it is blind. Yet, counting everything in sight, the United States government has less than twenty aircraft. In an encounter with a modern power we would be left standing as helpless as a blind man.

The United States has five aeroplanes in the navy, twelve in the army, and two in the national guard.

We should have 1,000, but neither the army nor navy departments have sufficient appropriations to equip themselves at present. Until there is a more liberal budget we shall have to depend upon private initiative. In France, Germany, and Italy there was a development of the air service by citizens, but our government hasn't the excuse that the European governments had. The military aeroplane was a guess in those days. Experiments were necessary and there was time. Today the aeroplane is an accepted fact.

Hereafter the aeroplane is a part of preparedness. Against a European power we would only be on a level if we applied our best and most vigorous efforts studying the air and training thousands of men as observers and pilots, in the regular army as well as in the militia. Against Mexico we would be fighting at a distinct advantage, and the period of bloodshed would be shortened for both sides as a result.

Until the government takes up the development the United States will have to depend upon volunteer services from the rich young men. Aeroplaning should take the place of following the hounds, of polo or big hunting. It is just as strenuous and sufficiently dangerous. It takes money, sporting instinct, and patriotism.

———

TAXATION OF GREAT WEALTH

December 19, 1915

The federal income tax law of 1894 had been declared invalid in 1895 by a 5 to 4 decision of the Supreme court. To overcome the court's objections, the 16th amendment was approved by congress in 1909. The income tax was instituted in 1913, the year the amendment was ratified.

A few years later, in the first world war, the income tax exemption was dropped to $1,000 and the maximum surtax was 65 percent. In the second world war, the exemption was dropped to $500 for those without dependents and the maximum surtax was 91 per cent.

Secretary McAdoo's report contains a recommendation for an amendment of the income tax law which shall provide that any one having a gross income of $3,000 a year shall make return. At present the net income is the test, and the change, Secretary McAdoo believes, "will result in a great increase in the number of voluntary income tax returns and in the amount of revenue that will be collected by the government." A recommendation for the direct reduction of the exemption to $2,000 is not made in the report but has been tentatively proposed.

THE TRIBUNE believes an energetic opposition should be developed to any increase of the income tax downward. If, as seems apparent, larger revenues are needed, especially for national defense, they should be obtained by increasing the burden of the rich, not that of the industrious men of small means. This class already bears a share of the public charges proportionately to their means much larger than do the rich, especially the very rich, and if there is any broad public policy underlying our federal taxation it will tend not to the enlargement of the contribution of the man who toils with hand or brain day by day but of the man whose wealth includes a very large increment from the labors of others.

The income tax as now applied is very largely a tax on the salaried people, who are not organized economically or politically. But their interests and democratic policy require that our tax legislation do not take advantage of that fact.

As THE TRIBUNE has said repeatedly, our income tax law and such inheritance tax laws as the states have adopted are not drastic as to great wealth. The graduation of the surtax is curiously moderate. But both the needs of larger revenue and the needs of larger democracy demand that the surtaxes shall be increased rather than the incidence of the regular tax broadened. The average man contributes directly and indirectly enough and more than enough to the upkeep of government. Let great wealth bear a larger share of maintaining a system which has made vast amassments possible. In our day we see the opportunities for the mass of men decreasing in range and variety and possibilities. We see wealth becoming more concentrated and less responsible in the hands of a growing class which has not earned it and which gives no service in return for the privileges enjoyed. A parasitic class is a focus of social infection, and if we have democratic foresight we shall treat it with courage and vigor. The standard of financial ambition has gone up with alarming rapidity. A millionaire is now merely a man of moderate fortune. The moral atmos-

phere of a very large class of Americans is being poisoned by an inordinate desire for the possession of enormous wealth, for the insolence of power, for the lust of luxury and display.

This phenomenon is an alarming fact in American life, and if we will learn from the experience of other ages and peoples we will not delay to deal with it.

The present congress should not fail to make this a principal subject of deliberation. Let us have a larger surtax on huge incomes and a federal income tax which shall carry out thoroughly the same social policy.

NOBODY HOME IN CALIFORNIA

November 10, 1916

Wilson was reelected in a close contest, the outcome of which was not certain until the second day after the polls closed. Only then, the returns from outlying counties in California swung the state definitely into the Democratic column. The editorial, with its reference to "the champion boob state," drew impassioned rejoinders.

California is the state which every now and then causes the rest of the nation to wonder how the trouble it makes can be safely handled. California hates the Japanese. It offends and insults the Japanese. It pays no attention to the treaty obligations of the United States.

Several times California in a stubborn and belligerent mood has almost put the alternative of war or

83

humiliation up to the rest of the nation. Some day, when Japan is ready, a California offense will result in the seizure of the Philippines and Hawaii.

California makes the trouble and expects the rest of the country to protect it. It may make a war and drag the rest of the country into it. California is our junker state in all except willingness to strengthen the ability of the federal government to meet the trouble it may make and is perfectly willing to make.

California ought to have given the Republican ticket a great majority. A state which demands the privilege of making trouble ought to be willing to meet it. It ought to be willing to take ordinary precautions against consequences.

California now seems to be concerned chiefly for the right to bluster. The moral condition of some little rotten spot in the interior of the United States can be understood. But California presents a long coast line which it demands that the United States defend. It wants a Pacific navy. It seems to have voted for a pacific navy.

How a state which when it is not scared to death itself is scaring the rest of the nation to death could have given even two votes in a precinct to the administration which maintains Josephus Daniels as schoolmaster of the American navy is a question beyond normal intelligence.

By giving Wilson the vote it did, California, with its record and Wilson's record, presented itself as the champion boob state of the American republic.

The only thing needed for the perfection of the irony was that the workers who want Japs excluded, in order that American standards of comfort shall not be lowered, should have tried to deliver the state to the administration which has tried to break down national courage.

California, which wants everything for itself, is inclined in the direction of an administration which blandly says that America demands nothing for itself that it does not demand for the rest of humanity. What a sweet vaporing of magnanimity for California to snuff up eagerly—California, which wants nothing more for itself than it wants for the Japanese!

The state which has put the nation on the edge of war several times, kept it in suspense for forty-eight hours in the election when the issue was one which should have been decided in this outpost state in two hours.

Some day California may have a Japanese governor—for a while. The rest of the nation eventually will annul his commission, but he may be there for a while.

If California gets its Japanese governor there may be men in California who will recall that in a time of national emergency they voted for the candidate of the party which wishes to be just as sweet to the rest of humanity as it is to California.

One of Kipling's characters, a chaplain with a burr under his tongue, quoted: "Quem Deus volt perdere, pr-r-rius demenstat," which, translated, means: "When people insist upon getting it in the neck they are first made dead from the neck up."

84

PRIZE FIGHTING

December 9, 1916

Prize fighting was legalized in Illinois 10 years later, in 1926. The Golden Gloves tournaments for amateur boxers, foreseen here, were instituted in 1928.

The sentiment which prevents prize fighting in this state is a symptom of a national disease—weakness, abhorrence of force, evasion of violence, love of softness.

This sentiment needs a corrective. It cannot safely govern in the United States. A more rugged conception of life must prevail unless the American character is to be hurt and made unfit for moments of national trial.

Life is not a soft thing. It is not tender. It requires hardihood, endurance, courage, and fortitude. It demands physical as well as moral stamina.

The continued avoidance of shocks is not a preparation for the inevitable consequences of living. The most prominent aspect of American life as it is being developed is softness.

Prize fighting is objectionable only as it is crooked and as it is made purely a hippodrome affair. It may be impossible to get the crooks out of the game. It certainly will be impossible to get rid of them so long as fighting has to sneak its way by respectability.

If respectability conceded the value of fighting, fighting might become respectable. We use the phrase prize fight to take up the challenge of the sentimental in its crudest terms. There is no use in raising an issue and being afraid of language.

There is mighty little value in a prize fight except as an incentive to the thousands of amateurs who would like to box.

If boxing should be legalized in this state there will be prize fights and the exceptional skill of the men engaged professionally naturally will stimulate the ambitions of rugged amateurs who, given opportunity, will box.

We are not interested in seeing that gladiatorial shows are provided for the scum of the city's population. We are interested in having a manly sport recognized. If a dozen youngsters of many hundreds or thousands survived the preliminaries and entered the semi-finals of a sparring contest we should know that a good sound sport was being used for the physical betterment of the young manhood of the nation.

Col. Garrity of the Second Illinois regiment says that his organization will give its best support to the attempt to obtain a law permitting glove fighting. We are with Garrity in this matter. The state may not be able to eliminate all the crooks in the fighting game, but it can try. It can try to get rid of the scum that covers boxing and fighting gloves.

If respectable sentiment will allow itself to be formed in favor of fighting and if it will recognize that there is nothing morally wrong in the spectacle of two willing young fellows hitting each other, the sport may be cut from its disreputable associations.

Americans cannot afford to become ninnies and mollycoddles. It will be a spiritual, moral, and physical disaster if they do. There is more immorality in softness than there is in violence. Force is the law of life. It is force which shoots the blade of grass up through the stubborn clay. It is force that cooks the steak. It is force that makes a man. It is force that makes a nation.

When respectability sets its face against force it becomes decadent. It seeks feebleness and soft luxuries. It becomes unfit for life. It is exposed in its feebleness to viciousness, which always tries to remain strong and courageous.

In the conflict between decency and viciousness, decency starts with the handicap, self-imposed, of being namby-pamby. Decency cannot physically cope with viciousness because decency has been misled to think that violence is wrong and viciousness knows that it is effective.

We are for legalized fighting in this state. The nation is bound to tire, sooner or later, of soft muscle reform. Soft muscle reform produces nothing but mushy minds.

"HAIL AND FAREWELL"

June 9, 1917

A tribute to the First division which could not be referred to by name in the editorial because of war-time censorship. The fate that awaited the division was accurately foreseen. Between Oct. 23, 1917, when its units first were engaged, and Nov. 11, 1918, the First lost 4,996 killed and 17,324 wounded.

Pershing is in England and the American flag is drawing nearer the hot pit of hell in France. Events have made beggary of the imagination and have filled American prospects with promises and threats which could not have entered the comprehension even a year ago.

This is the greatest flight the American eagle ever made, flying over the heads of American soldiers, greater than the flight to the Philippines and to China, greater in its significance and in its certainty of sacrifice.

The men who will follow Pershing over sea and into battle will carry the flag to the severest test it ever has had, a severer test than even it met at Gettysburg, but, we trust—we know—to the triumph it had at Appomattox.

These soldiers are the first offerings of the American nation to a cause which we have made ours, in a struggle which we might have avoided by compromise of self-respect, honor, and highest interest.

They are the first of this generation's sacrifices for the next, the first pledges of honor. They are the videttes of a great army. When they take their stand in France and look towards Germany it will be as if a few horsemen had come up on the crest of a hill, visible to the enemy as the forerunners of great hosts far in the distance, there unseen and unheard, but coming.

Pershing's men to the Germans are these forerunners of a new enemy. They appear at the top of the hill, few in numbers, not tangibly menacing, but terribly suggestive. It is not what they can do which will be significant. It is what they mean, what they promise, and what they threaten.

In numbers they are less than Gen. French's "miserable little army." But Germany has met the great armies which followed those British troops. The miserable little army was sacrificed, but the ground where the men died will, we think, see other British soldiers, and the German mind may comprehend that millions, if needed, carrying the same flag that Pershing takes to France, will see the ground where his men die.

It is with an unashamed emotion that we think of Pershing's men. They are our first sacrifices. The regular soldier—the confession now humiliates the nation—has never been close to the affections of the American people. He has been respected for efficiency and used. He has done his work well, and, we believe, cheerfully. But there has been no fondness in the nation for him.

Now it would be a dull and crabbed nature which could contemplate without emotion the picture of this expedition. It is the last expedition for most of them. The duty which they undertake will take them. It is in a real sense a sacrifice which should be close to the heart of the American people. It is to stimulate them to comprehension and realization and to nerve them to action.

Pershing's casualty lists will be the first rap of the hand of fate on the American door, and fate will come later with equal foot to the door of the rich and the door of the poor.

These soldiers are the consecration of America to a cause, its pledge of duty, its token of good faith and determination, of fortitude, resolve, and courage.

There are Englishmen who cannot control themselves to speak of the lost expeditionary force. There will be Americans who will not be ashamed to demonstrate their emotion over the first sacrifice.

Pershing's men will go silently and the nation will have no opportunity for demonstration. But there are roses in their rifles just the same.

THE LIQUOR TRAFFIC

July 11, 1917

The 18th amendment was approved by congress on Dec. 17, 1917, and was ratified on Jan. 29, 1919.

At the request of a subscriber, this editorial was reprinted on June 11, 1932, with appropriate comment. The later editorial appears on Page 107.

If the secret records of the brewing and distilling industry were ever brought to light they would tell a story of social and political corruption unequaled in the annals of our history. If the veritable narrative of the American saloon were ever written it would make the decadence of Rome look like an age of pristine purity in comparison.

Whisky, wine, and beer never caused half as much injury to society as the manufacturers and purveyors of these beverages. If these men have not made a practice of committing murder and arson it is because these crimes did not seem immediately profitable. The liquor business has been the faithful ally of every vicious element in American life; it has protected criminals, it has fostered the social evil, and it has bribed politicians, juries, and legislatures.

The inherent corruption has extended even to the so-called decent saloon. There are few that do not serve adulterated products and it is an unusual proprietor that is not more pleased when his patrons are getting drunk than when they keep sober. Philip Drunk stays longer and spends more money than Philip Sober. That is one reason why the saloon would rather sell ardent spirits than beer; they are more intoxicating.

We have been speaking of the "decent" saloon; the other variety is almost unspeakable. The smallest count in the indictment against the evil barroom is its persistent evasion of the law. We are not surprised to read that numerous Cook county roadhouses are operating without licenses, that they keep open on Sunday, or that they seem to exercise a mysterious control over public officials. Yet these are only minor offenses in the calendar of saloon iniquities.

The brewers have at times tried, or said they would try, to clean up the saloon business. The head of a great St. Louis brewery often told his confrères that it was the brewers' only salvation. The theory was accepted but the practice was always to expend every energy to sell one more keg of beer, even if it had to be sold to bootleggers and resort keepers.

It is for these reasons that the prohibition movement has gained such strength. The demand for the abolition of the liquor traffic is the expression of a ripening conviction that it is conducted by nefarious means for nefarious ends.

"After us the deluge" seems to have been the philosophy of the liquor men—but now the deluge seems to be on the point of breaking.

A MESSAGE ON THE TREATY

June 30, 1919

THE TRIBUNE *had made public the text of the Versailles treaty, one of the great scoops in newspaper history.*

Here the Editor finds he cannot share President Wilson's belief that a new order in international affairs has been created. "A very old order, the order of Adam. . . . will continue to rule the affairs of the world."

President Wilson has taken the occasion of the signing of the treaty of Versailles to send to the American people a message upon that much mooted instrument. We should like to share Mr. Wilson's enthusiasm for the treaty. We wish that it might prove to be all that he claims for it. But we are not as much impressed by his confidence as we might be if our observation of the course of events at the conference gave his eloquent periods more support. The treaty of Versailles will prove to be "a great charter for a new order of affairs in the world," there can be no doubt of that, a new order in the Adriatic, in the Balkans, in Asia Minor, in central Europe, in Shantung and Siberia and Africa. But what the new order will be lies in the bosom of Providence.

Mr. Wilson's aspirations are likely to take in public utterance the form of assertions having more the tone of certitude than, perhaps, he intends. This is a familiar device of

88

leadership, but it is not a basis of cool judgment in public opinion or in the formulation of policy.

For example, when Mr. Wilson declares that the treaty "ends, once for all, an old and intolerable order under which small groups of selfish men could use the peoples of great empires to serve their ambition for power and dominion," we must beg leave to take the assertion in a poetic if not a Pickwickian sense. Mr. Wilson has been very emphatic about old orders and new orders, but we have been conscious throughout his career as a maker of international policies that he is disposed to ignore one order, a very old order, the order of Adam, which under many appearances and mutations will continue to rule the affairs of the world long after Mr. Wilson has taken his place in history. "Small groups of selfish men" have dealt with the fate of other men since the world began and we see little in Europe or in the particular arrangements of the treaty of Paris to give basis for Mr. Wilson's confident assertion that henceforth they are to be helpless. The conference was unable to protect the millions of Shantung and we see no reason why the same great powers working under a different name but by no means altered in interests, ideals, purposes or powers, will now transform themselves and the order of affairs which brought forth this peculiar flower of justice and peace.

In THE TRIBUNE published on the day in which news of the signing of the treaty came to us appeared a very interesting dispatch from THE TRIBUNE's Paris correspondent,

Henry Wales, giving the terms of a treaty proposed one month before the signing of the armistice. The parties concerned were Japan, Germany and Russia, and the object was an alliance among those great powers to offset the alliance of Great Britain, France and the United States. Without accepting this treaty, on the evidence as yet available, as authentic, we would refer to it at least as expressing the possibility which has pressed upon the Paris conference and which, it is believed in well informed quarters, had much to do with those concessions to expediency which, though Mr. Wilson does not recur to them, are most candidly inconsistent with his theory of a new order of affairs in the world.

Examined with neither cynicism nor evasive optimism, the treaty of Versailles must seem to most of us to promise an order of affairs which is indeed new in its rearrangement of power, but which is in many essentials as old as Europe. It is important, if there is any considerable measure of truth in this view, that the American people, unused as we are to old world problems, look straightly at the facts of the new order rather than accept blindly any zealous claims of Utopian accomplishment.

––––

THE PHILIPPINES: A STRATEGIC WEAKNESS

October 17, 1920

A forecast of Japanese strategy in the war that came 21 years later.

The Democratic policy as to the Philippines has favored granting independence at the earliest practicable moment. The Republican policy has been considerably less radical and has contemplated at least a long term of dependence if not permanent incorporation in the American system.

We think the late war has brought about a change in the Pacific which makes it advisable to review and perhaps recast Republican policy respecting the islands.

The most important change, relevant to our Philippine policy, is the taking over by Japan of the island groups formerly held by Germany north of the equator. These islands lie between the Philippines and America. Japan has taken them as mandatory under the league of nations, but we shall be foolish indeed if we cherish any doubt that the islands have become permanent possessions of Japan. They will be quickly populated and organized by her and they will be fortified. In fact, there is report that already a fortified naval base is being prepared.

In case of war between Japan and the United States, the Philippines would be at once cut off from us. Expert opinion predicts that Japanese strategy would isolate them and strike at Hawaii or the canal. If our fleet were divided as it is now a naval victory over the Pacific fleet would probably result in the capture of Hawaii, the strategic key of the Pacific, and with the route from the canal flanked from that point and in the former German islands, notably the easternmost, the Marshall islands, the Philippines could be taken at leisure.

The defense of the Philippines would involve a large naval and military force and would hardly be worth while, especially if we propose presently to give them up. At present they greatly increase our responsibilities and weaken our strategic position in the Pacific by drawing on our limited naval and military resources.

THE TRIBUNE correspondent at Manila believes that the Japanese will wait until the trained soldiery of this war have got past effective military age, relying upon American pacifism and optimism to prevent the training of the younger men and the maintenance of an adequate military and naval establishment. The Japanese are thoughtful and far-sighted and we fear they are right in expecting that we shall do as we have done after every war, reduce our defenses to a minimum. They will do no such thing and as a result their organized strength will increase as ours decreases. They will make good use of their strategic gains and when they are ready and we least ready they will strike for mastery of the Pacific.

If these are plausible ideas of the possibilities or probabilities of the future, why should we burden ourselves with the Philippines, which may cost us Hawaii, almost an essential to the defense of our own shores and the canal from attacks from the west?

We are not aspiring to prophecy or to dogmatize. But here is some matter worth thinking over. We cannot afford to drift. If we do we shall pay for our indolence in unnecessary sacrifices of good American blood and perhaps serious loss in national position.

UNREGENERATE EUROPE

November 13, 1921

The article appeared as the delegates to the Washington disarmament conference were assembling.

It is natural that pacifists and excited humanitarians should stress the evil consequences of the world war at this time. It is equally natural that foreign| statesmen and public agencies should join them in keeping this phase of the European situation before us. It gives a tremendous momentum to the pacifist propaganda, and it relieves the governments and peoples of Europe of a large part of their responsibility for the present condition of their affairs.

But the American mind should clear itself on this point. No one will deny that the war is responsible directly for a vast wastage of life and property. But what needs recognition and emphasis at this moment, and from the very beginning of the conference, is that had common sense and self-control governed the policies of the governments and the sentiments of the peoples of Europe their affairs would not be tottering now on the rim of chaos.

On the contrary, were there wisdom and courage in the statesmanship of Europe, were there the same selfless devotion in chancelleries and parliaments as was exhibited on the battlefield, Europe would have been today well on the way to recovery.

The expenditures of the war and the intensification of long existing animosities and jealousies undoubtedly have complicated the problems of statecraft and of government. Undoubtedly the temporary depletion of man power and the temporary exhaustion of body and spirit among the war worn peoples were a burden which recovery has had to assume. Undoubtedly the wastage of wealth and diversion of productive agencies were a handicap to expeditious restoration.

But that these are chiefly responsible for the present state of Europe we do not admit and the future judgment of history, we are confident, will deny.

It is chiefly the folly which has been persistently demonstrated by governments and people since the war that is responsible for Europe's condition today. It is because the moment hostilities ceased and the enemy was disarmed, victors and vanquished turned their backs on the healing and constructive principles they had solemnly asserted from time to time when matters were going against them at the battle front, that the European nations almost without exception have been going down hill. There never in history has been a more perfect illustration of the ancient sarcasm: "When the devil is sick, the devil a monk would be; when the devil is well, the devil a monk is he."

If we wish to know why Europe is in the present state, we cannot do better than to draw a parallel between the assertions of purpose and principle of the allies and "associated" powers in 1916, '17, and '18, and what has actually happened since Nov. 11, 1918.

The war was a gigantic folly and waste. No one will deny that. But it was not so foolish nor so wasteful as the peace which has followed it. The European governments, those who come at our invitation and those who remain away, would have us believe they are mere victims of the war. They say nothing of what the war did for them. We might remind them that they profited as well as lost by the war. Many of them were freed from age long tyranny. They got rid of kaisers and saber clattering aristocracies. They were given freedom, and their present state shows how little they have known how to profit by it. They have been given new territories and new resources, and they have shown how little they deserve their good fortune. The last three years in Europe have been given not to sane efforts to heal wounds, remove hostilities, develop cooperation for the common economic restoration which is essential to the life of each. On the contrary, they have been marked by new wars and destruction, by new animosities and rivalries, by a refusal to face facts, make necessary sacrifices and compromises for financial and economic recovery, by greedy grabbing of territory and new adventures in the very imperialism which brought about the war.

It is well for Americans and their representatives to keep this in mind. The appeal to America's disinterestedness is unfairly fortified by the assumption that Europe is the innocent victim of one egotist's or one nation's ruthless ambition. We can take due account of the disastrous effects of the Prussian effort at dominance, but that should not overshadow the stubborn errors which began over again on the very threshold of peace, and which have made the peace more destructive than the war. When the European governments and peoples are ready to make a real peace, which cannot arrive until they give over the policies and attitudes that produced the world war, America will then not fail to give generous aid. But America would be foolish to contribute to the support of present methods or give any encouragement to the spirit which now prevails in the old world.

ABOLISH "PITTSBURGH PLUS"

April 22, 1922

The campaign was carried to a successful conclusion. "Pittsburgh plus" was ended in 1924 by an order of the Federal Trade commission, with which the United States Steel corporation promptly complied.

THE TRIBUNE today adds a new plank to its platform for Chicago: Abolish "Pittsburgh Plus."

To the casual reader, and even to the average business man, the importance of this plank may not be apparent. The fact that E. H. Gary, chief of the United States Steel corporation, characterizes the fight to abolish the system as the greatest lawsuit ever tried in this country may impress the public with its importance. The fact that it involves an amount probably exeeding $75,000,000 annually may add to the realization of its importance. The fact that every builder or renter of a structure in which steel is a material, that every user of machinery or any product of machinery, that every traveler on concrete roads, that every person interested in any way in the prosperity of Chicago pays toll to the "steel trust" through the "Pittsburgh plus" practice may convince the public that the subject is one demanding interest and the fight against it is one demanding support.

The campaign to abolish the "Pittsburgh plus" system, under which all rolled steel sold anywhere in the United States is priced according to the Pittsburgh mill price plus the freight rate from Pittsburgh to the point of destination, has tremendous backing. The Western Association of Rolled Steel Consumers, the Southern Association of Rolled Steel Consumers, the American Farm Bureau federation, the National Association of Purchasing Agents, civic and commercial organizations in a dozen cities, the legislatures of Illinois, Wisconsin, Minnesota, Iowa, and Missouri, and the senate of Georgia have all declared against the practice as abusive, unfair, and a menace to the prosperity of their membership and their districts.

The federal trade commission is now conducting hearings on these complaints. Every day facts are being brought out which reveal the damage which the system is doing to the prosperity of Chicago and the middle west. For instance, R. R. Robertson, president of a Chicago concern which uses 6,000 tons of sheet steel annually, testified Thursday that he has been virtually barred from Indiana and Ohio markets because he must pay an imaginary freight rate from Pittsburgh to Chicago and a real rate back to those markets, while Pittsburgh manufacturers, getting their material for $7.60 a ton less than he pays, can easily undersell him.

That is typical. The manufacturing business of Chicago is placed under a tremendous handicap. The entire prosperity and development of the city is impeded. We gain nothing from our proximity to the great steel mills of the Calumet district, paying the same price for steel if we back our trucks up to their loading platforms as we should if we had it shipped by rail all the way from Pittsburgh.

The practice began shortly after Andrew Carnegie made Pittsburgh the center of the steel industry in 1880. It became firmly established with the advent of the United States Steel corporation in 1901. It subsidizes the manufacturers of Pittsburgh at the expense of the entire middle west and puts 75,000,000 unearned dollars annually into the pockets of the steel makers. When freight rates were low the tax on western builders and manufacturers was less. Now it ranges from $7.60 a ton at Chicago to $13.20 a ton at Duluth, despite the fact that Duluth manufactures steel.

There is no excuse for it except the "steel trust's" desire for profits. E. H. Gary himself in a speech at Duluth in 1917 said both Gary and

93

Birmingham made steel for less than Pittsburgh. His figures, reduced to percentage, showed that steel was made at Gary for 18.12 per cent less than at Pittsburgh. The corporation's chief defense is that the system stabilizes the market and that Pittsburgh, adjusting the balance of supply, is entitled to dominate the field and fix the price. Such a contention on its face is economically unsound. Furthermore, it is probable that if the Calumet, Duluth, and Birmingham mills were allowed to produce to capacity they would more than supply all needs, and the Pittsburgh balance of power would be eliminated.

The practice is so obviously unsound and discriminatory against Chicago and the middle west that it must be abolished eventually. THE TRIBUNE purposes to exert its best efforts to hasten that day. Every medium of publicity and public or private enterprise in Chicago should be glad to join in the battle.

THE CONSPIRACY THAT FAILED

April 20, 1923

The first of two leading cases on freedom of the press won by THE TRIBUNE. See, also, the editorial of June 3, 1931, commenting on the decision of the United States Supreme court in Near v. Minnesota.

A unanimous decision of the Supreme court of Illinois puts an end to the ten million dollar libel suit brought by Mr. Thompson's administration in the name of the city against THE TRIBUNE. It defeats the most remarkable attempt to suppress free speech in the history of the American press. If the attempt had succeeded the constitutional guaranty of a free press might have been erased from the fundamental law for it would have become an empty phrase.

The attempt was a tribute to the daring and ingenuity of the Thompson regime. Its theory need not be discussed here since the opinion of Chief Justice Thompson has been published in full. But the political circumstances of the litigation should be remembered by the people of Chicago. The suit was a formidable device to crush criticism of misgovernment. No newspaper lacking in resources of defense could withstand such an assault. The damages claimed were so large that even THE TRIBUNE would have been seriously injured if they had been imposed, and undoubtedly the politicians who invented the case hoped that exposure of city conditions and criticism of city hall maladministration would be checked if not completely paralyzed by the mere threat implied in the litigation.

But this suit was only a part of the drum-fire of lawsuits directed against THE TRIBUNE and other Chicago newspapers which were attacking the Thompson regime. Besides the ten million dollar libel suit in the name of the city, there were personal suits in the name of Mayor Thompson claiming damages in a total of approximately $3,000,000.

We know of nothing like this campaign in our political history and it was only one phase of a strategy directed at the suppression of press criticism. The Thompson organization controlled not only the city administration but the official machinery in charge of elections, and as a political organization it set forth to control the judiciary. It nominated a slate of henchmen for the judicial elections and tried to put them on the bench. There was a civic revolt against that sinister assault and it was overwhelmingly rebuked at the polls, but had it succeeded the newspapers of the city which were exposing the city's deplorable condition under the Thompson regime would have been at the mercy of judges subservient to that regime.

The people of Chicago ought to realize the narrowness of their escape from a domination of predatory politics freed from the only restraint it has seriously to fear, the restraint of exposure and criticism protected by the constitutional guaranty of freedom of speech and of the press.

To control the courts and then to crush the press by almost confiscatory litigation was the plan of the late city hall regime, and nothing more dangerous was ever devised in our politics.

When the history of the Lundin-Thompson regime is reviewed, it is clear that its strategy was governed by this central object, the suppression of the press. Thompson's perpetual theme on the stump was "the trust press." Without facts, and indeed in defiance of well known facts, he concentrated on the persistent effort to discredit the newspapers which were exposing the evils of his administration. And

realizing that this would fail in due time, the effort to discredit was supplemented by an effort to suppress by means of litigation in courts controlled by the city hall organization.

The people of Chicago should remember these facts against a time when the men identified with the policy of the Lundin-Thompson regime seek to regain power or other men borrow their strategy. There is no defense of the city from predatory politics if the press can be either controlled or bludgeoned into silence. The great conspiracy of the Lundin-Thompson regime against the rights of free speech has dismally failed, but its significance should never be forgotten in this community or in any city of the country.

AS EXPECTED, BRYAN WINS

July 22, 1925

Mr. Bryan survived the trial by only a few days. Mr. Darrow died in 1938. Young Mr. Scopes took his doctor's degree in geology at the University of Chicago and for many years has been employed as a field geologist. The Tennessee Supreme court found that the judge had erred in that the state constitution required fines in excess of $50 to be assessed by a jury rather than by a judge. The legal record ends there because the defense was left without anything to appeal and the state did not renew the prosecution. Judge Raulston was defeated when he sought reelection. The so-called monkey law is still in force.

Young Mr. Scopes, who taught a high school class something which Mr. Bryan says is antagonistic to

95

belief in the divine creation of man, has been found guilty by the jury in the Dayton, Tenn. court. He is fined $100 for that. The court held that the law was valid. The jury held that Scopes had violated it. That phase of the religious trial is over. The defense wanted to lose the case to carry it up for final decision on its issues. That opportunity now is presented.

In its essence it was a religious trial. Technically Mr. Scopes was not on trial because he had any particular religious belief or opinion, but he was on trial because Mr. Bryan and the people influenced by him had a particular belief and opinion. The United States Supreme court, if the case reaches it, may find that the people of a state have the right to forbid or order in their public schools any kind of teaching they see fit. It has already found that they may not compel people to send their children to public schools, which saves the day from the worst which might be accomplished otherwise by the influences successful in Tennessee. The country is almost certain now to find a widespread attempt to enact religious law, essentially if not technically religious law, putting the state behind a certain set of beliefs in one fashion or another.

Judge Raulston in the trial of Scopes had decided that the testimony of the scientists and modernist theologians was irrelevant. They were not allowed to take the stand to explain what science teaches of the universe and its origins and developments and how modernist religion accepts this. That seemed to settle the trial both as an occasion of

exposition and as a show. But it didn't.

The judge decided that the attorneys for the defense and the prosecution could put each other on the stand and write their own tickets so far as questioning went. Court adjourned to a platform on the lawn to keep from falling into the cellar under the weight of the assembling populace. Clarence Darrow called Mr. Bryan as a witness and, although the proceedings had a new foundation, the lid was off. A rare event.

Mr. Bryan stood pat. He is a fundamentalist. He believes that Eve was made from Adam's rib, that the serpent was condemned to crawl on its belly and eat dust because it enticed Eve to the apple, that women suffer in bearing children as punishment of the whole sex for all time because Eve tempted Adam to eat the apple. He does not know where Cain got a wife, but he knows there was one. He believes the flood killed all living things except the things in the ark and probably fish outside. He believes that was 4,262 years ago.

He believes that the confusion of tongues was the result of the attempt to build the tower of Babel and because of that some people speak English, some French, some German; because of that we have all the varieties of cultural languages and primitive tongues.

Mr. Bryan's one departure, under questioning, from his otherwise literal reading was in an idea that the days of creation might have been periods instead of days of twenty-four hours each. He believes that a big fish swallowed Jonah and retained him three days. He believes Joshua made the sun stand still.

Both he and Darrow were red with anger at times, but Bryan repeatedly said that no notorious agnostic such as Darrow would have the privilege of saying that Bryan had been afraid to submit his belief to questions or had dodged one of them.

Mr. Bryan's position in a land which has tried to preserve religious liberty was almost impregnable. When he says he believes a thing and that it is his religion he is unshakable. Most decent people in normal life and in ordinary intercourse would not say anything to him in question of that belief. Many people who look to the Bible for inspiration and good counsel, or for evidence of divinity and immortality, do not believe as Mr. Bryan believes, but there are not many of them who would scoff at him if he held to his belief or if he expounded it.

Mr. Bryan was at Dayton, not to defend his right to have and expound these beliefs, but in furtherance of his plan to put the power of the state behind them. In each state in the Union he wants a law which will bring the aid of the legislature, the law, the courts and police to the upholding of his way of reading the King James version of the Bible.

Thus far he has succeeded in getting only negative law. That is law which prevents the teaching of anything not in accord with the Biblical narrative of the divine creation of man. But it would be useless for him to say that he will not go further if he can. He recognizes certain limitations. He cannot get a law compelling the teaching of his belief to every one in a state, but at none of the stages leading up to the compulsory adherence to his interpretation of the scriptures could he stop if his conscience is as active as he says it is and if his conviction is as profound.

He not only ignores everything which science has learned of origins, but he ignores the whole history of revealed religion, all the investigations and interpretations of its learned men of all ages. He has a story and the nation shall stick to it. It shall have legislation and authority back of it.

That was the start of colonial government in New England. Adams' "Emancipation of Massachusetts" reveals the worst of it, the killing and torture which maintained a theocracy and the interpretation of revealed religion satisfactory to that theocracy.

The nation can stand it if one state has a vagary in legislation affecting education. Nature can take her course. But we are not going back to the theocracy of Massachusetts Bay colony under the Puritans and we'll not without a fight have the public school system of the United States supporting Mr. Bryan's beliefs with the public money, the courts, and the police.

THE TRIBUNE AND PROHIBITION

October 12, 1925

"We concluded at length that we could afford the luxury of expressing an opinion. . . ."

Something over four years ago this newspaper took its stand against

97

prohibition by constitutional amendment. The decision was not an easy one to take. THE TRIBUNE had never been a wet newspaper, and it did not want to be considered a wet newspaper in the sense in which that phrase was understood at the time. The editors of THE TRIBUNE, then as now, believed liquor bad for men and women. We feared that if we attacked constitutional prohibition and the rigors of the Volstead act we should inevitably be accused by many of our readers of advocating the use of intoxicants. How thoroughly justified that fear was the readers of the Voice of the People column know.

Four years ago, when the decision was taken, THE TRIBUNE had a circulation around 480,000 daily and 800,000 on Sunday. The backbone of its circulation was the prosperous home owning, church supporting citizen. We knew what that kind of man and wife thought of a wet newspaper, and in the long series of conferences that preceded our decision we were repeatedly reminded of the losses we should suffer in our choicest circulation should we decide to attack the prohibition law.

We concluded at length that we could afford the luxury of expressing an opinion which was held in any number of newspaper editorial rooms throughout the country, but, for one motive or another, was given almost no expression, particularly in the middle west. We saw that the amendment and Volsteadism were surely, if unintentionally, undermining the American idea of government. We saw the constitution, which had been intended to

specify the machinery of government and the inalienable rights of the citizen, converted into an instrument for regulating the private lives of the people. We saw the eighteenth amendment as a vicious precedent inviting to further tyrannies. We knew of the millions in the great cities who did not see any moral wrong in drinking, and we foresaw the failure of attempts to enforce the law on these unwilling millions. We feared corruption of public officials, but, we confess, we did not anticipate the extent to which bribery has reached in the intervening years. What alarmed us, probably more than any other single circumstance, was the attack in the Volstead act upon the orderly processes of justice. The jury trial was virtually abolished in liquor cases, and in its place was the injunction, to be followed by imprisonment for so-called contempt of court. All this we saw as a menace to the republic and we said so. We have continued to tell the story ever since.

We did not know what the response of our readers would be, but we were certain that if only half of what the drys claimed for the popularity of their cause was true we were in for some dark days. We had had experience with advocating unpopular causes, and it was not a pleasant one for those whose livelihoods depended upon the prosperity of THE TRIBUNE. You may advocate popular causes without gaining readers, but when you advocate unpopular ones you stand an excellent chance of losing them.

We do not insist, then, that the phenomenal growth in circulation of

THE TRIBUNE since we took our stand against prohibition is to any considerable extent the result of our opposition. Rather it is proof that the prohibition cause is not dear to the hearts of the people of this community. If it were, our circulation would have dropped. Instead it has grown faster than the circulation of any long established newspaper has ever grown over a period of years. We do not think the increase in the Sunday circulation from 801,000 in September, 1921, to 1,020,000 this September is so significant in this connection as the increase in strength of the daily paper from 483,000 to 658,000, a gain of 175,000, or 37 per cent in four years. The Sunday edition is part magazine and part newspaper. The daily edition is all newspaper, and it must grow or decline on its merits as a newspaper. If any considerable part of the population of Chicago and the neighboring states had been outraged by our viewpoint we should have lost rather than gained.

There is a lesson in this for the politicians who vote dry but drink wet. They can vote as they drink and they will not suffer for their sincerity.

AN ELECTION TALK WITH TRIBUNE READERS

April 12, 1928

In line with the policy laid down by Joseph Medill, THE TRIBUNE has not been slavish in its Republicanism. It was the chief influence in driving Lorimer from his seat in the senate as it was also the principal opponent of Small, the corrupt Republican governor of Illinois, and of Thompson, the corrupt Republican mayor of Chicago. This editorial deals with the downfall of Small.

THE TRIBUNE feels that there has been a political reassociation of it and its readers and that it took place in time to avoid an intolerable situation and avert unendurable consequences.

It should be apparent that this newspaper and the citizens have in the main the same purposes with respect to public life and government. The object is the maintenance of praiseworthy administration and honest legislation. It is not of primary importance what particular persons shall be given authority and responsibility, but that the persons so trusted shall be competent and willing to conduct public affairs honestly with regard to public funds and successfully with regard to public security.

There will be differences of opinion as to public policy, but THE TRIBUNE and a majority of the citizens of Illinois at no time have opposite views of what are the elemental requirements of government in the state. In supporting these requirements, THE TRIBUNE has tried to inform and persuade, having in the very nature of the newspaper business larger opportunities to gather information than are possessed by the body of citizenship.

A general recognition of the community of interests and purposes came just in time to put Illinois back on its balance when it was in danger of a complete collapse. The confident rascals of Illinois were convinced that they were protected from public displeasure and could definitely count on approval of whatever outrage they wished to perpetrate against public security, public money, political rights, and the life and property of the individual.

They had combined privileged corporate wealth and privileged vice and crime in an organized effort against public rights, public morals, and public security. They had given privilege to one and immunity to the other and were taking toll from both in return. Thus organized, they were seeking an indorsement from the people, either deluding them or frightening them into compliance on the one hand or submission on the other. A success meant that Illinois and Chicago were distinctively disgraced, dishonored, and endangered in the American commonwealth and that in this state there was the greatest failure of democracy the republic had known. Suppose, in retrospect of a genuine calamity avoided and for guidance when danger recurs, as it may, we consider a few of the circumstances.

In preparation for Tuesday's election, Gov. Small had required the legislature to pass a bill repealing the section of a state law by which his tenure of office could be attacked in the courts and he be removed because he had cheated the state and taken its money.

State's Attorney Crowe, with Small's assistance, had put through an act restricting the calling of special grand juries.

LEN SMALL, who was seeking renomination to the governorship in the 1928 Republican primary, was defeated by Louis L. Emmerson.

Samuel Insull had invested $158,000 in the political aspirations of Frank L. Smith, the chairman of the Illinois commerce commission, and $35,000 in William Hale Thompson's political organizations. Samuel Ettelson, from Mr. Insull's law firm, the firm through which political investments had been made, was Mr. Thompson's corporation counsel. The street car bills for a perpetual franchise were drawn in Mr. Insull's law offices and given to Ettelson in the city hall. They had failed once in the legislature, but Small had promised Thompson, Ettelson, and Insull to call a special session of the legislature after the primaries to pass them. An increase in elevated fares had been applied for before Small's commerce commission.

We are repeating these facts because they, with others, cumulate to show the people of Illinois what they confronted and what they smashed. Small had gained immunity. Crowe had usurped power of prosecution. Thompson had the police force. Small had the pardoning power. They had the legislature in subordination. The money had been paid in the traction deal. It was waiting a rape of the election for its fulfillment.

With control of pardons, police, and prosecution, the combination, having made its arrangements with public utilities, made its other necessary arrangements with crime and vice. The campaign was to be terrorized. It was to be dominated by machine guns and bombs. Precincts were to be carried by killers, gamblers, procurers, and male brothel house keepers. They were to take

100

their profits out of the degradation of city morals. They were to intimidate the decent citizenship. They were to keep people from going to the polls. The murder of Esposito, the bombing of the home of Judge Swanson and the attempt on his life, and the bombing of the home of Senator Deneen were announcements of what vice and crime had been turned loose to do in the precincts April 10.

THE TRIBUNE confesses that here was something in truth terrifying. This newspaper had fought the growth and development of it, but in twelve years it had reached further out each year. The checks which could be given it were impermanent. For reasons which in themselves were dismaying, THE TRIBUNE could not bring a majority of the voters of Illinois to see what frightful consequences they were bringing down on themselves by their refusal to protect themselves in their elections.

People even took some satisfaction in seeing the failure of just newspaper criticism and of self-evident facts. If that was to continue, the immunity of reptilian politics was found in the very exposure of criminal acts and it was the critic who was in danger and not the criminal.

Any one who saw the thugs and killers of the criminal world and the creatures of vice come out into the open Tuesday at the polling places or patrol the streets in cars with guns knows that this danger was not theoretical or rhetorical. The stake was enormous. The plunder was so rich that it invited any desperate

act to lay hands on it.

The question was whether in this primary election there would be a repetition in results of the previous campaigns in which a strange blindness or perversity of opinion would protect the most dangerous combinations of politics and crime which ever threatened an American state. It seemed incredible that such could be the case, but what was there in experience to create real confidence that it would not be?

It may be confessed now that THE TRIBUNE undertook this renewal of its fight against this heretofore successful alliance with the prospects of having to protect its own personnel if the people gave another vote of confidence in the combination which controlled police, pardoning, and prosecuting authority. There was no protection for any citizen in that case who exposed the villainies of Illinois and Chicago politics or who opposed them.

Government for the guaranty of rights, the protection of life, and public security would have disappeared. Opposition would have been handled with machine gun fire and bombs. A disclosure of rascality would have been followed by an explosion at the front door. Political opposition would have been quieted with sawed-off shotguns. Reputable citizens would have been slugged at the polls.

It was against this that the voters arose in a storm of indignation, in a return to old-time savvy in voting, in protection of themselves and their institutions.

We think it is fair to say that if THE TRIBUNE was right this time in

101

its advocacy of principles against rascality, it was right before when it opposed these men and exposed their acts. It is probably true that the public mind responds slowly. In that there may be an instinct for fairness, but it influences unwisely when it gives protection for destruction of government.

With this accomplished revolt of Illinois citizens, Illinois seems a cleaner state and certainly is a safer one.

FALL AND HIS BACKGROUND

November 11, 1929

Secretary Fall's debt to the Ohio gang; and the Ohio gang's debt to the prohibitionists.

Albert B. Fall, sentenced to a year in jail, with a fine of $100,000, is the first member of a President's cabinet to be found guilty and ordered punished for a crime involving his official position and duty. He was convicted of a felony in leasing the Elk Hills naval oil reserve to Edward L. Doheny, from whom he had accepted $100,000.

Fall was secretary of the interior in President Harding's cabinet. He was not the only one of that President's appointees and subordinates to be touched by scandal or charged with malfeasance or crimes against the public.

It may never be proved, but it has been suspected in a line of plausible reasoning, that much of what happened after Harding's inauguration was planned before his nomination and that his nomination was contingent upon agreements such as produced the naval oil reserve scandal. Certainly, without loss of time, steps were taken which would indicate a prearrangement.

It may not be proved that the death of Jake Hamon of Oklahoma, killed by his mistress, removed the man who was to have taken the part afterward played by Fall in the Department of the Interior, but such a probability has been in the thoughts of many American citizens who know something of what went on in Chicago at the time of the National Convention which nominated Harding.

Harding was a product of Ohio politics. He had one hand reached out to the group of Ohio politicians later known collectively as the Ohio gang. With the other he was in fellowship with the political clerics who had brought religious organizations into political action. Ohio was one of the first states in which it was discovered by unscrupulous men that a combination of religious professions and corrupt practices could go far and safely.

Ohio, with the headquarters of the Anti-Saloon league at Westerville, had produced a school of politics which perfumed rascality with the odor of sanctity and which found protection in the political pew. This scheme of combining the lip service of religion with the expert use of burglar tools had the approval of the Ohio moralists and prohibitionists, because it enabled them to use the politicians for the one purpose they had in mind, the coercion of government.

The church congregations of the United States are for honesty in public life and incorruptibility in

public office. The political clerical-
ism which works with corruptionists
betrays the instinctive desires and
the confirmed wishes of the people
of the congregations. The object of
the political cleric is a control of
political action for his purposes and
the spoils politician barters a vote
for a character indorsement.

These considerations may be taken
into account in the case of Mr. Fall,
the only cabinet minister ever convicted of a crime committed in office.

THOMPSON

April 9, 1931

THE TRIBUNE *threw all its weight
into the effort to defeat William
Hale Thompson (1869-1944), the
corrupt Republican mayor of Chicago. Thompson served three terms as
mayor: from 1915 to 1923 and again
from 1927 to 1931. After his death in
1944, his safety deposit boxes were
found to contain $1,484,750, most of
it in cash, the profits of his political
career.*

William Hale Thompson was defeated Tuesday after a campaign
which he alone made disgraceful.
The election was an ejection, a dirty
job, but Chicago has washed itself
and put on clean clothes.

Thompson recognized THE TRIBUNE
as his chief enemy. THE TRIBUNE was
glad to earn that opinion. It certainly tried to do so. It has taken
the fight to him on every occasion
during the long and depraved course
of his administration. It is un-
pleasant business to eject a skunk,
but some one has to do it.

For Chicago Thompson has meant
filth, corruption, obscenity, idiocy
and bankruptcy. He has given the
city an international reputation for
moronic buffoonery, barbaric crime,
triumphant hoodlumism, unchecked
graft and a dejected citizenship. He
nearly ruined the property and completely destroyed the pride of the
city. He made Chicago a byword for
the collapse of American civilization. In his attempt to continue this
he excelled himself as a liar and de-
famer of character. He's out.

He is not only out, but dishonored.
He is deserted by his friends. He is
permanently marked by the evidences of his character and conduct.
His health is impaired by his ways
of life and he leaves office and goes
from the city the most discredited
man who ever held place in it.

THE BACKGROUND OF THE GAG LAW

June 3, 1931

*J. M. Near and Howard A. Guilford
in September, 1927 founded a weekly
newspaper in Minneapolis, known as
The Saturday Press. Two months
later, the county attorney, alleging
the paper to be malicious, scandalous,
and defamatory, asked that its publication be enjoined. He was acting
under the terms of a Minnesota statute
adopted in 1925. In due time the injunction was issued.*

THE TRIBUNE, *recognizing the threat
to the freedom of the press implicit in
the Minnesota law, undertook the appeal. The Supreme court of Minnesota sustained the injunction but it
was declared invalid and the law
which authorized it unconstitutional
in a 5 to 4 decision of the United*

103

States Supreme court. Near vs. Minnesota (287 U. S., 697) *has become a leading case on freedom of the press. Guilford was murdered in 1934.*

The full force of the decision in the Minnesota press suppression law is not likely to be realized without reference to the conditions from which this remarkable piece of lawmaking sprang. The dissenting opinion leaves the impression that the issue involved merely the proper method of suppressing a business regularly producing malicious, scandalous and defamatory matter. The actual situation in which the legal controversy has risen is not disposed of on such easy terms. The gag law is but an incident in the political, economic and social history of Minnesota and its full significance cannot be grasped without reference to that history. It is the history of a long struggle for domination by powerful and ruthless private interests over law and government in that commonwealth.

In its earliest stages the state was ruled by the lumber and iron barons, who were bent upon an unrestrained exploitation of the great natural resources of Minnesota. The control of the politics and machinery of government was essential to their freedom to exploit, and the profits of this exploitation gave ample means to purchase the control. But control for their own predatory freedom necessarily involved the allowance of freedom to political and official allies. This is a rule without exception in the strategy of corrupt power. The interests which sought freedom to exploit on a large scale could not afford to fight other less "respectable" forms of exploitation. Doubtless they would have indulged in an inexpensive civic morality, "compounding for sins they were inclined to by damning those they had no mind to." But this is not practicable.

The result was, and always is, that the great powers controlling through their wealth and unscrupulous ability were enforced allies of the lesser grafters in local government and police who fattened in comparatively modest proportion upon the illicit appetites and desires of people, on the wages of sin, on commercial vice, on gambling and the political grafts of public administration. Read the chapter on Minneapolis in Lincoln Steffens' "The Shame of the Cities," if you would have a concrete picture of this phase of the problem of good government in Minnesota.

In due time came a moral reaction in the body politic against this situation, but not unnaturally it struck at the central and greater evil, the domination of the great interests which possessed the real power over the state and directed its control. Unhappily this revolt took the form of political and economic radicalism and fell into the hands of demagogues and self-seeking individuals who borrow idealistic formulas to disguise their own personal ends and utilize the force of public indignation to acquire power and place. The Minneapolis police under the radicals was as vile as if not more vile than it had been under the Big Money Rule.

With both factions devoted to corruption in its varying forms, the only great and persistent danger to either party was and is publicity and plenty of it. Thus while the reactionaries devised and enacted the gag law it was the radicals, come into power, that used it to suppress the Saturday Press for exposing the corruption of the police under radical rule and forcing the dismissal of the chief of police.

No inkling of this background of the gag law will be found in the dissenting opinion. On the contrary, its implication is, as we have said, that there was involved only the suppression of an abuse of press freedom. But the Saturday Press was not suppressed for the lies it told. It was suppressed for the true stories it printed of official perfidy. It was not suppressed because it was scurrilous, recklessly defamatory, abusive, and incendiary, but because, whatever the character or motives of its editor, it was giving publicity to conditions which political profiteers and corruptionists could not afford to permit the public to realize.

This is no novel development. The whole history of censorship gives it meaning. Every effort to restrain and suppress utterance by political dictatorship, save in time of national peril, has been on behalf of a political tyranny which dared not submit its cause to the conscience of men.

We may say on behalf of Justice Butler, a Minnesota man, and on behalf of the Minnesota judges who upheld the gag law, that living in and through the economic and political conditions we have referred to they have some reason, though we trust not a conclusive one, to give way to a feeling that conditions in Minnesota are inevitable and that unqualified defense of American principles by violent or vigorous journalism was damaging to the fundamental interests of that commonwealth. We think such an attitude is mistaken and mischievous. It could have been pleaded in extenuation of every reactionary judge in our history from Jeffreys to Taney.

THE TRIBUNE's intervention in the Minnesota cause was prompted by its own recent experience of an attempt to suppress public disclosure through another piece of legalistic sophistry—"the municipal libel suit" —by an equally corrupt and demoralizing city government. That attempt was defeated in the Illinois Supreme court, whose opinion, delivered by former Chief Justice Thompson, is a landmark in the law of free press. The notable opinion of Mr. Chief Justice Hughes in the Minnesota case is still another of even wider authority, and it should arrest, if it does not end, the efforts to cripple the guarantee of a free press, which have of late been an ominous resort of unscrupulous power disguised in the guise of almost every fad, faction, and schism known to politics.

As for the community directly concerned, the people of Minnesota, it is to be hoped the severe reproof administered to their legislature and to their Supreme court will not only instruct them in the nature of free government, but will awaken them to the character of the political forces which govern them.

F. ROOSEVELT SEES A MAD SCRAMBLE TO CUT

April 22, 1932

In the Hoover administration, as the depression deepened, THE TRIBUNE pressed with growing vehemence for the reduction of federal expenditures. Candidate Roosevelt took the same line, to his great political advantage, but in an unguarded moment he revealed his true feeling on the subject. He was promptly taken to task. Two months later Mr. Roosevelt won the nomination, and pledged himself again to a regime of economy.

Gov. Roosevelt says that "in the mad scramble to cut" the costs of government "there is danger that some of the humanitarian work carried on by the government may suffer to such an extent that future generations will be seriously affected." As he was addressing the International Society for Crippled Children his plea was especially that "those seeking to cut the cost of government do not lop off the essential aid for the crippled child."

This is very characteristic of Gov. Roosevelt, both of his amiability and of his political tendency.

When Gov. Roosevelt speaks of "the mad scramble to cut" he reveals significantly his own secret attitude toward retrenchment and his inability to understand the critical problems of public finance. If he can see "a mad scramble to cut" at Washington he has a very peculiar vision. What the phrase really means is that Franklin Roosevelt is for plenty of spending by the government.

Of course, pity for crippled children is a commendable emotion, also an almost universal one. But that the care of crippled children is a proper responsibility of the central political agency, the federal government, is quite another question. When Gov. Roosevelt protests against lopping off "the essential aid for the crippled child" he begs that question. Federal aid for the crippled child, as Gov. Roosevelt knows, is not "essential." It is a very small part of the great work for crippled children carried on in the country by medical science and philanthropy. But by calling it "essential" he implies that any one who favors retrenchment in this case is so inhumane as to be willing to leave the crippled child without aid.

The superficiality of Gov. Roosevelt's thinking is well illustrated in this speech. It reveals his complacency toward the continued inordinate expenditures of the government and his inability to foresee its disastrous consequences. The conspicuous reluctance of both the executive and the legislative branches of government to reduce expenditures becomes in Roosevelt parlance "the mad scramble to cut." That is because he favors bureaucratic expansion and huge federal expenditures and the nation should understand that if he is elected President his influence will be persistently in that direction. In the guise of humanitarianism or public welfare the march of paternalism will go on with his encouragement and help.

As for crippled children, those who more wisely regard their welfare will not be deceived by the notion that a federal bureau is "essential" or that government expenditures which are rapidly bringing it to bankruptcy promise anything but a national misfortune in which the aid of all suffering will be stricken. The best hope of crippled children and of all the humanitarian activities of the nation is in the restoration of public and private solvency and prosperity.

If the American people want more taxation, more bureaucracy, more regulation of their affairs by officials, more centralization of power at Washington, Franklin Roosevelt is their man.

_____

EVILS OF THE LIQUOR TRAFFIC

June 19, 1932

The earlier editorial to which reference is made appears on Page 87. The 21st amendment, repealing the 18th, was passed by congress on Feb. 20, 1933, and was ratified on Dec. 5 of the same year.

An Iowa reader requests us to republish a TRIBUNE editorial of July 11, 1917, "in the interest of fair play." We are glad to do so. It will be found on this page under the heading Editorial of the Day. It is an appropriate heading, for THE TRIBUNE would not change a word of it today. Its republication is "in the interest of fair play," though not as implied by our correspondent. In the interest of fair play it will serve to remind our readers that contrary to the innuendoes and charges of dry fanatics THE TRIBUNE never condoned the evils of the saloon or of the liquor traffic. On the contrary,

it exposed and excoriated them, as this reprinted editorial illustrates. Not content with exposure and criticism, THE TRIBUNE was the first metropolitan newspaper, if not the first of all American newspapers, to expel liquor advertisements from its pages.

THE TRIBUNE did not believe in prohibition. It advocated effective control by the states with effective control of interstate transport by the federal government. It did not believe in the efficacy or propriety of federal prohibition, but it did not oppose the experiment. It limited itself to discussion of the pros and cons and hoped for the best, though even that effort at reasonable discussion was bitterly resented by prohibitionists.

In this course THE TRIBUNE was mistaken. If it had foreseen more clearly the results of the experiment, if it had considered the constitutional issues involved more thoroughly, it would have fought with all its power against the adoption of the prohibition amendment. But, like most Americans, THE TRIBUNE was preoccupied with the great war and its editors were in the army. It preferred to wait, though not with confidence upon results. We waited until the conditions created by prohibition convinced us that it was a major error of American policy. That conviction has grown clearer and stronger with us as with what we are confident is a great majority of the American people. With us, as with them, opposition to federal prohibition no more implies approval of the evils of intemperance or of ill regulated and unscrupulous traffic in intoxicants than any condemnation of a greater evil implies approval of a lesser. With reasonable people the fact that we do not like the bubonic plague does not mean we like smallpox. The evils condemned in the editorial of 1917 have been followed by worse under prohibition.

It is only bigotry that can ascribe to the great body of American citizens who oppose the prohibition regime a disposition to condone the evils which existed before the adoption of the 18th amendment. We demand its repeal because it has brought even worse conditions than those we attacked in the past. We demand its repeal because there are other methods of dealing with the evils of the traffic in or use of intoxicants, methods consistent with American institutions and principles, less demoralizing in their effects upon government, society and the individual, and more efficient in restraint of the evils of intemperance.

THE PRESIDENT ACTS

March 7, 1933

Mr. Roosevelt's handling of the banking crisis wins commendation. The temper of the new congress is correctly appraised.

The President has acted with admirable promptness. He has seen the immediate situation truly and has taken emergency measures required to meet it. But now, as always, the final responsibility rests upon the American people. If, as we have every reason to believe, they will meet the crisis in the spirit in which the President has met it, there will

be a minimum of disruption of industry and commerce. If the people yield to fear, resumption of normal business conditions may be needlessly delayed.

A frightened man can be counted upon to do one of two foolish things. Either he will thrash about in a panic of activity or he will run and hide. Translated into the terms of the present crisis, that means that the coward will either attempt to hoard money, or supplies, or both; or will lapse into a complete funk, refusing to believe that the present difficulties will lift within a few days. Both procedures can only result in a prolongation of the present troubles. What is needed above all else is the calm assumption on the part of the American people that the crisis is temporary and that the proper course of conduct is the normal course. Normal buying, normal credit extensions and normal confidence in the future will do a maximum of immediate good. Conduct born of fear can only hamper the President, the treasury, and the banks in their task of restoration.

The firmness which has been displayed in Washington is most reassuring. If Mr. Roosevelt had not issued his decree suspending specie payment and placing an embargo on gold there would have been something to worry about. The fact that he acted without shilly-shallying indicates as plainly as anything can that he knows what it is all about and is not afraid to take drastic action for the protection of the people of the United States. If either measure had not been adopted the result might have been such a drain on the country's gold stock as would have made the task of reorganization infinitely more difficult. As it is, we have an immense stock of gold and we have it where we want it, in the vaults of the treasury and the federal reserve banks, where it can serve the needs of the whole nation rather than of a few frightened individuals.

The confidence which the President engendered with his decree was reinforced by his summoning of congress to meet before the week is out. This provides a measure of Mr. Roosevelt's political astuteness. He is not afraid that congress will get out of hand. He knows that a new congress, meeting in the midst of a crisis, must accept his leadership, not only because a congress containing so many new faces must be without its own leaders for a time but also and more especially because public opinion now will force congress to do promptly what it might dawdle with for months under less trying conditions. This is the golden moment to slash expenditures and place the treasury in an impregnable position. There is no doubt that congress will follow the President and, on the basis of his exemplary management of affairs thus far, no doubt that congress should follow him unhesitatingly.

_____

GERMANY AND THE NAZIS
September 19, 1933

Hitler became German chancellor on Jan. 30, 1933.

Hitler's Germany is surrounding itself with unfriendly and apprehensive neighbors. The opinion of the world is again turning against the Germany of chauvinist enthusiasms, persecuting zeal, and repressive and provocative government policies. The legend of Teutonic fury, widespread during the war, but later modified by the moderateness of the German republic, is being revived to the detriment of the nation in the thought of the rest of the world. Again it seems probable even if incredible, that the Germans in control are determined to face their future with the rest of the world aroused against them. And again the rest of the world tries to understand the contradictions of a people who produce so much that is admirable, humane, scholarly and intelligent, distorted by so much that is furious and disturbing.

In many respects German government produces a genius of lawful order, stability, honesty, and respect for the common good, justly admired by other people who have found it more difficult to obtain these virtues of administration from their own political action. These German virtues were found in the smaller political units such as the municipalities and some of the constituent states. It is the German nationalist who is now obsessed by the mystic puerilities of Hitler and who gives alarm everywhere by the excesses of speech and action.

A German protesting against severe criticism and condemnation of the present state of his country might say that the rest of the world drove him into these courses, and he will not be easy to answer. Certainly he was promised more than he was given. Mr. Wilson, ap-

109

parently speaking for all the enemies of monarchical Germany, told the German people that, once they dethroned kaiserism and set up democracy, a friendly world would welcome them without a reproach and without an injury. They accepted this word as good and tried a liberal government of the people. They found that the word was not good. It wasn't a responsibility of the peacemakers that Moscow attacked the new republic on every open front, but it was the fault of the peacemakers that the Germans who might have resisted this found themselves constantly weakened by peace conditions imposed on them. The feeling grew that if Germany did not succeed in resisting it was doomed to an inferiority which would destroy the spirit and strength of the people. These fears may not have been justified in any long view of the future, but they could undermine government in Germany, which seemed to be accepting such consequences.

Hitler and the excesses of his Nazis may be the products of the treaty of Versailles. If so, that does not make the folly wise or brutality condonable. But it spreads responsibility into quarters which must assume a share of it, although it cannot relieve the present governors of the German people from facing their accountability if the consequences of world criticism and opposition have serious effect. No one who has any hope for the future of organized society can believe that the brutal, liberty destroying governments of absolutism to which so much of Europe has turned as to a new model can prevail. They too much

degrade individual worth and too much destroy the value of life as modern man has learned to demand it. Society under the terror is a plunge backward into miseries from which humanity has struggled too long to escape. Confidence in the future must assign this new type of savage emotionalism and mailed fist to a passing insanity, caused by fear and temporarily powerful fallacies.

————

POT AND KETTLE
September 26, 1933

An early recognition of the essential quality of totalitarian rule.

The communist demonstration before the German consulate in Chicago was intended to suggest to the unthinking that what Hitler favors the communists oppose. The truth of the matter is that in most essentials the Nazis and the communists think alike. They both deify a central government. Both prevent free criticism and the organization of a political opposition. Both exercise a rigid control over the printed and spoken word. Both deny that the individual has any rights either of life or property which must be respected. The principal difference between them is that Stalin speaks Russian and Hitler speaks German.

Stalin says a man with two cows is an enemy of society and sends him off to forced labor in the arctic. Hitler says a Jew is an enemy of society and enforces a boycott against him. Stalin says it is a crime, punishable by death or exile, to question the wisdom of the communist party.

110

Hitler says it is a crime, punishable by imprisonment in a concentration camp, to question the wisdom of the Nazis. There is little or nothing to choose between these doctrines and policies. The explanation of all of them must be made in terms of ignorance and mental disorder.

THE FIRST TEST OF THE NEW DEAL

March 14, 1934

On Feb. 9, 1934, the post office cancelled its contracts with the commercial air lines for carrying the mails. Fraud and collusion in the negotiation of the contracts were alleged. On May 8, following the tragic incidents mentioned here, the commercial lines resumed the service.

After three weeks of the new deal in the air mail, in the course of which ten army pilots lost their lives, the service was suspended. The country was thus temporarily deprived of the only important improvement in postal delivery instituted since the railway mail service was organized.

The New Deal in its entirety is a miscellany of experiments and expedients. Of all of them, the new deal in the air mail is the only one which, by its nature, could be fully tested in a short period. Some time must elapse before the results of the AAA, the NRA, the devaluation of the currency and kindred measures can be placed before the American people for appraisal. The cards have been dealt at many tables, but only at the air mail table have they been played to the last trick.

The results are there for any one to see. The usefulness of the air mail is to be narrowed. Ten army pilots have been needlessly sacrificed. The money changers who somehow managed to anticipate the news that the commercial lines would lose their contracts have banked handsome profits. The phenomenal progress of commercial flying in this country has received a severe check and hundreds of men have been thrown out of work in consequence. All of these items are on the debit side. There are as yet no credits.

The tragic failure of the new deal in the air mail does not, of course, prove that the wasteful slaughter of the little pigs, the plowing under of cotton, the repudiation of the government's solemn promise to pay its debts in gold, and all the other hasty improvisations are doomed to produce similarly unexpected and undesired results. But the air mail fiasco does throw a great light upon the expectable consequences of impulsive, inadequately considered government by administrative decree. The fiasco does underline the maxim that haste makes waste. It does emphasize the truth that self-righteousness and emotional fervor are not substitutes for thought and accordingly frequently lead to undesired consequences.

In this connection it is worth remembering that almost without exception every item in the bundle of improvisations called the New Deal was conceived in haste, in an atmosphere of emotional excitement. The measures have been put into operation by a group of men and women who regard themselves as the chosen

111

leaders of the new Zion. Under these circumstances the outcome of the New Deal in its first completed test must be regarded as more than a little significant.

STOCK EXCHANGE REGULATION

June 4, 1934

By this time, THE TRIBUNE, *as the previous editorial discloses, was more than a little skeptical of the New Deal. There were a few items in Mr. Roosevelt's legislative program, however, which were favored.*

The federal regulation of stock exchanges which will shortly be instituted may encourage some people to think that most of the risk has been removed from the business. The truth is that the purchase of securities is inherently a speculative venture. There never was a security the value of which (measured by the price some one is willing to pay for it) did not fluctuate in greater or less degree; and there never will be as long as we live in a world in which men and institutions are born, grow old and die, a world many of the forces of which are unknown and unpredictable. The fact that a commission is to be appointed to regulate stock exchanges cannot prevent prices from falling when sellers outnumber buyers.

Banks failed despite federal and state supervision. Depositors who had assumed that any government-supervised bank was safe were taught a costly lesson. There is real reason to fear that a somewhat similar experience may be in store for the public under the new stock market regime. Prospective purchasers may be encouraged to think that regulation will prevent, if not all fluctuations in prices, then, at least, all violent fluctuations. There is no reason whatsoever for holding this view. On the contrary, there is actually some reason to fear that price movements will be more erratic than they have been if regulation results, as many expect it to, in reducing the volume of transactions. The smaller the volume, the greater the influence on the market of a given transaction.

Regulatory commissions are at best a slender reed. They are not all-good, to say nothing of all-wise. All commissioners are not always honest and all are not always competent. It is by no means certain that in another speculative frenzy such as the one which was reaching its climax five years ago the commissioners would have either the vision or the courage to defy the almost universal belief that a New Era had dawned. There is no certainty, either, that in a falling market the commissioners might not seek to arrest the decline before it had run its full course.

This is not to say that the act is without its merits. In so far as it puts the force of law behind measures calculated to preserve a free market in securities, the act is useful. To the extent that it prevents manipulation and encourages honest corporate reporting and a true sense of trusteeship on the part of officers and directors, the measure may prove useful. If it does not operate to shut off credit from industry, as many fear it will, and if it does not raise a false confidence in the stability of security prices, the law may prove of considerable value, assuming that the men who are chosen to do the regulating are carefully selected for character and experience.

———

A WARNING FROM GERMANY

July 2, 1934

THE TRIBUNE was, perhaps, the first publication to recognize the danger to freedom of the press implicit in the proposed NRA code for newspapers. THE TRIBUNE and its editor in his capacity as chairman of the American Newspaper Publishers' association's committee on press freedom, were surely the most persistent and outspoken agents in defeating the draft favored by the administration. Some newspapers were at first more than a little reluctant to risk the wrath of a powerful, vindictive, and immensely popular Executive; and some others supported the President and Gen. Johnson in the long and bitter controversy. As stated in the editorial, however, the great majority of editors and publishers were steadfast in demanding the reservation.

Enemies of Hitler will speak of the events of the week-end in Germany as murders and assassinations. Apologists for Hitler will reply that he has been obliged to take strong measures to preserve order. Students of political history will regard the argument as fruitless. They will recognize what has happened in Germany as the expectable consequence of any dictatorship and the inevitable consequence of a dictatorship which has disappointed or angered a considerable number of the people subjected to it. They will recognize, also, that the killing has only begun. Bloodshed begets bloodshed.

Hitler rose to power after an election in which he and his political allies obtained a bare majority of the popular vote. His government was by no means the unanimous choice of the German people. To consolidate his position he was forced to still all the active and latent opposition. He did so by taking over or suppressing all opposition newspapers as well as the radio. At the same time he proscribed all opposition parties. Freedom of the press, freedom of assembly, and the right of the German people to petition for the redress of grievances were ruthlessly denied. Religious tolerance ceased. Suspected opponents were jailed without being told why and in hundreds of instances without the barest formality of a trial.

Though its means of expression were gone, the opposition persisted, as it always will where men are not slaves. No two men see exactly eye to eye and, of course, no nation of 60 million people can be expected to do so. The opposition in Germany has been gathering strength of late through the failure of the Hitler dictatorship to fulfill its promise of a prompt solution of Germany's economic and financial difficulties. Under such circumstances, courageous men will conspire to overthrow the dictatorship and will be joined by ambitious men eager to succeed to positions of power.

113

The world does not yet know what the opponents of Hitler intended to do, if, indeed, their plans had matured to the point where overt action was contemplated. What is abundantly clear is that in the absence of any means of expressing their dissent they could resort only to inciting defection in the armed forces and to assassination. When the press is fettered, the machine gun and the bomb replace it as organs of opinion. Hitler knew that he had left his opponents no other course of conduct and, in the logic of absolutism, his decision to strike first was strictly correct. Mussolini may have counseled his action, but Hitler probably did not require the advice. He preserved his government in the only way that a dictatorship can be preserved.

If a nation wishes to avoid the horrors of civil uprising it must avoid dictatorship. Americans who have observed with growing alarm the spread of absolutism in many quarters of the globe read the news of the week-end in Germany with foreboding. Can we avoid the dictatorship which inevitably leads to ruthless killings? The answer is that we can if we will but recognize the trend toward dictatorship in time to repudiate it.

Fortunately, the trend is easily recognized. The most important of the means of expression is the press. It is, therefore, the touchstone. Governments which seek to restrict the freedom of the press are moving in the direction of dictatorship. No dictator has ever permitted free expression of opposition, and none ever will. A man with dictatorial ambitions will always strive to suppress the voices of his opponents and thus prevent them from rallying their forces. He will not fully achieve his program of suppression until he has engineered his coup d'etat, but he will show the bent of his mind in his pronouncements to and about the opposition press.

In the light of events in Germany, the American people dare not defer a candid appraisal of our administration. The preservation of the republic demands an examination of official pronouncements and official acts to determine our government's attitude toward freedom of expression. Such an examination will show that the government has sought to prevent opponents from enjoying the use of the radio. The government, not content with its control of the radio, has just taken over the control of all other forms of electric communication, with all that that implies of control of opinion. The government did seek by every means in its power to keep out of the newspaper code a clause specifically reserving the constitutional freedom of the press. When this effort failed because of the foresight and determination of editors and publishers throughout the country, the President expressed his intense irritation in words scarcely less vehement than those of his subordinate, Gen. Johnson.

It should be unnecessary to add further items to the record. There is no lack of them. The evidences of trend are as unmistakable as they are ominous. This nation has received its warning. Will it apply the brakes in time to avoid the precipice?

114

THE GOVERNMENT TRIES TO MAKE A DEAL WITH THE TRIBUNE

July 6, 1935

Those were grave days, but occasionally their gravity was relieved by incidents such as the one described here.

For a month and a half officials of the United States treasury department, assisted by the United States army, have been unsuccessfully conducting negotiations for a purchase from THE TRIBUNE. The price is not in dispute, the method of delivery is not an issue, and there is no question of title. The deal is being held up by the insistence of the government that as a condition of sale we agree to abide by undisclosed and undetermined restrictions the government may enact into law despite a holding by the Supreme court that the government has no constitutional power to do so. The completion of the transaction has also been deferred because of the unwillingness of THE TRIBUNE to spend several dollars to fill out forms, statements, and vouchers when the amount involved is only 40 cents.

We are terminating the negotiations because of the expense of carrying them on. A government with everybody's wealth to snatch a share of, and the unrestricted use of bond and currency printing presses at its disposal, is able to produce the money to pay the cost of letters and telegrams and miles of red tape on a 40 cent transaction. But a private business which must out of its own efforts find the wherewithal to carry on, must eliminate needless correspondence and simplify its processes. If we did business with all of our million customers on the basis on which the government conducts its activities we couldn't last a week, or the paper would sell for $2 a copy.

On May 23 the treasury department sent us a number of forms asking for a bid to supply one copy of the booklet containing charts reprinted from the financial section of THE TRIBUNE. The booklet is for sale for 40 cents at THE TRIBUNE Public service office, 50 cents by mail. When John Gillespie, manager of the public service office, surveyed the mass of government printing and realized the amount of paper work he was asked to do he wrote the treasury advising that since the amount of the transaction was small, to avoid bookkeeping and billing costs it would be more simple to send 50 cents in stamps, or 40 cents and a franked envelope.

To this the treasury replied, acknowledging receipt of a "bid," but neither accepting nor rejecting it. Instead the treasury asked to have incorporated in the "bid" and "contract" a statement that if subsequently legislation along NRA lines is enacted, whatever it may be, we would agree to abide by it. The Supreme court decision outlawing NRA and the codes had been handed down on May 27 and the treasury was attempting to accomplish by indirection what the Supreme court said the government had no authority to do.

Mr. Gillespie again replied, pointing out that it was only a 50 cent transaction—40 cents if no stamps were required—and for the treasury

115

to send along the stamps and never mind the rigmarole. On June 26 the war department came into the negotiations. The signal corps of the United States army delivered a wireless message asking for an immediate reply by wire advising whether we agree to the inclusion in a contract of a statement that we will abide by subsequent legislation along lines described in their letter.

The patience of Mr. Gillespie, which up to this time had stood up amazingly well in carrying on the trying negotiations, now was exhausted. He has replied to the latest message of the treasury and war department that if the government doesn't want to pay 40 cents for the book, cold turkey and no more monkey business about it, then the whole deal is off. Other departments of THE TRIBUNE which have cooperated in an advisory way feel the same way about it. For although THE TRIBUNE sells for only 2 cents per copy, 40 cents isn't such an extraordinarily large sum of money to us that we are willing to go to any lengths to acquire it.

THE BRITISH LOSE THE ETHIOPIAN WAR

April 5, 1936

The invasion of Ethiopia began on Oct. 3, 1935. On March 2, 1936 the last organized resistance to the invaders was overcome.

Ethiopia is conquered. The British empire is whipped. The fall of the former may appear in times to come as a minor incident in the development of a continent. The failure of the latter may appear as a major event in the dissolution of the most widely spread empire, long the greatest of world powers.

For important reasons given a moral aurora, Great Britain undertook to keep Mussolini from extending his African possessions. He was reaching for the headwaters of the Nile and he planned what he hoped would become a powerful and populous Italian colony along the trade route to India. Great Britain, which forty years ago invited Italy to go in and take it, became peremptory in saying that it could not and should not be done.

The British government staked prestige and power on this decision. It made a demonstration in force against Italy by sending its fleet into the Mediterranean. It brought the league of nations into action and imposed embargoes to force Mussolini to terms. It discharged a foreign minister, Sir Samuel Hoare, who tried to make a compromise and appease Mussolini with a part of the whole.

Thus Great Britain closed the road to retreat, hoping probably that if both commands and sanctions failed, Ethiopian climate and topography might win. All failed, and the mistress of the seas could not stop a military enterprise requiring as it did the transport of men and supplies overseas. The affair was right in the lap of sea power and the great sea power failed, unable to accomplish its purpose by demonstrations of force and unable to go to extremes.

It may be that the British, making

the best of a bad situation, will console themselves with a bit of Ethiopia in the Lake Tsana region if they can get it. A property gain will hardly compensate for a loss of prestige in world affairs. Great Britain's position is not that of a boss nation. The Italian accepted the dare and took the best his European opponent tossed at him. He comes out winner.

The British dominions, which the world war found closely cemented in the empire with great respect for the governing class and a proper colonial regard for London, are now on their own, held only as and when and how they will. In the colonial wars preceding the American revolution the colonial soldiers learned that they had little to learn from the British army. They ceased being impressed. They were not afraid to try conclusions. They did and won.

The troops from the dominions had somewhat the same experience in Europe in the world war. They came to regard themselves as better than the troops from Great Britain and to prefer their own commanders to British generals of great name. Close association produced a tendency to separation and the British did not oppose the separatist desires, a wise decision, but not one preserving a closely knit empire.

Then after the war Ireland finally fought its way to freedom. The struggle of centuries was won by the Irish patriots. If the Free State does not satisfy the extreme Irish republicans it is at least the Free State and goes on its own and the British make few assumptions of authority. The developments as a whole may have been inevitable, but

they were nevertheless destructive of empire. The prestige and importance of the once dominant country in the imperial government waned. Now, defeated by Italy in a war of national wills, the British reputation as a world arbiter declines. It may be found later that these were the days in which a historic power closed the great pages of its career.

THE FUTURE OF THE SUPREME COURT

February 7, 1937

"Millions who voted for Mr. Roosevelt are due for a sharp awakening and it should not be long delayed" said the post-election editorial of Nov. 4, 1936. The awakening came on Feb. 5, 1937. when the President proposed a reorganization of the federal judiciary. The senate defeated the court-packing provisions of the bill on July 22, by a vote of 70 to 22.

For many years it has been THE TRIBUNE'S custom to defer comment on important state papers until at least a day has been devoted to study and reflection. The practice has its justification in ordinary circumstances, when the public has been prepared by hints and trial balloons for the official pronouncement. When, as on Friday, without any previous intimation of what was coming, the President sprang his proposal for amendment of the judiciary act, a postponement of comment was doubly merited.

Mr. Roosevelt's message and the bill which he submitted to congress to carry his ideas into effect propose

117

changes of two distinct sorts.

He asks, in the first place, for certain procedural changes in the administration of justice. Their purpose, as he explains, is to expedite justice in the federal courts. Under this head there is little that is novel and nothing of transcendent importance. The President has raised the question whether the creation of the office of proctor, the systematic transfer of district and circuit judges to courts which are overwhelmed with business, and the speeding of appeals involving constitutional questions will, in fact, expedite the administration of the law. Whatever the answer may be, the President's recommendations in this category involve no fundamental change in the spirit of our institutions.

The other proposed change is fundamental. Its objective is to enable Mr. Roosevelt to command a majority of the Supreme court. He has sought to create the impression that the two suggestions are one and that they stand or fall together, but obviously they do not. The question raised by his proposal to increase the membership of the Supreme court to a maximum of fifteen raises the question: Shall the Supreme court be turned into the personal organ of the President?

That is fundamental because, if congress answers yes, the principle of an impartial and independent judiciary will be lost in this country. In all probability it will be abandoned for all time. In the past other administrations and other parties in power have been dissatisfied with Supreme court decisions, but have abided by them rather than invite the consequences of a manipulated court. Mr. Roosevelt takes the opposite view. He places his immediate objectives above everything.

Once a President has packed the court to obtain the approval of a particular course of action which he favors it is as certain as anything can be that his successors will find the same or other ways of accomplishing the same end. The court will be manipulated again and again. The will of the people expressed in their constitution will no longer be the supreme law of the land. Confidence in the integrity of the law will be undermined and none of the rights of the citizens will be secure.

The change which Mr. Roosevelt has proposed is revolutionary. The word is used advisedly. The essential difference between free government in America and dictatorial government in Europe is the independence of our three branches of government. Mussolini dominates not only the executive branch of government but the law-making and judicial branches as well. Otherwise he would be no dictator. Precisely the same description applies to Hitler and Stalin. They are dictators because they write the laws, they put them into effect, and there is no independent judiciary to which the citizens can appeal against the autocrat.

Mr. Roosevelt is the chief executive by election, and he holds congress in the hollow of his hand. How lightly he regards its theoretical independence in framing the nation's laws is indicated by the fact that he gave congress a draft of his judiciary

118

bill with orders to pass it. If the bill is passed by a supine congress, as he expects, he will have control over the courts, too. From that moment the will of the President will be the constitution of the United States. And his successors will take the same view of the matter. Power once seized is seldom relinquished.

Tomorrow Mr. Roosevelt's successor may be the creature of a Ku Klux Klan party, with all the fanatical belief in racial and religious intolerance which goes with it. Racial and religious minorities in this country may well tremble at the prospect which Mr. Roosevelt has presented.

HE, TOO, WOULD KEEP US OUT OF WAR

October 6, 1937

The revelation that Mr. Justice Black who had taken his place on the Supreme bench on Aug. 17, 1937, was at one time a member of the Ku Klux Klan aroused intense public interest. Many commentators thought that when Mr. Roosevelt turned provocatively to foreign policy in his speech dedicating the Outer Drive bridge in Chicago, he was seeking to distract attention from an appointment which was proving of great embarrassment to him. THE TRIBUNE *took a different and much more serious view of the President's pronouncement.*

The crowd which gathered at the dedication of the new bridge yesterday heard Mr. Roosevelt deliver what may well prove to be the most important speech he ever will make.

Mr. Roosevelt announced a new foreign policy for the United States.

It would be more accurate to say that he readopted the foreign policy of Woodrow Wilson, the policy which brought the United States first into armed conflict with Mexico and then into the world war, the policy which was overwhelmingly rejected by the American people after the war.

Mr. Roosevelt, like Mr. Wilson, believes it is the mission of the United States to maintain the sanctity of international treaties; that it is our duty to side against the nation which our government deems to be the aggressor in war. Specifically, he indicates that the United States is in duty bound to take action of some sort against Japan for her war in China as well as against Italy and Germany for their participation in the Spanish civil war. He did not name these countries, but the inference was unmistakable in his reference to the nations which broke the league covenant, the nine power treaty for the protection of China and the Kellogg-Briand treaty for the preservation of peace everywhere.

We signed two of those treaties, he said, and having signed them we have assumed a duty to see that they are observed.

Mr. Roosevelt went a step further. He plainly indicated the line of action he intends to pursue to bring the treaty-breakers to their knees. We are to associate ourselves with the powers which abide by their word. He did not name the powers with which we are to join forces, but here, too, there was no mistaking his meaning. They are to be Britain, France, Russia, and any others

119

which can be persuaded to join the movement. We are to cooperate with them in a commercial and financial boycott of the aggressors. No other meaning can be placed upon his analogy of the imposition of a quarantine to guard against epidemics. War, he said, was like an epidemic. Its spread can be prevented only by isolating the victims of the disease, by having no contact with them until they are no longer carriers of the disease.

What happened at the headquarters of the league of nations at Geneva on Monday had its meaning clarified by Mr. Roosevelt's speech in Chicago on Tuesday. At Geneva the representative of China had requested the league of nations to declare Japan the aggressor, the legal preliminary to a boycott. That might have left the United States out, for the United States is not a member of the league. Viscount Cranborne, representing Britain, proposed a different course. Instead of invoking the covenant of the league, he said, let us invoke the nine power treaty. At Chicago Mr. Roosevelt seemed to fall in with this suggestion. If the boycott results from action under the nine power treaty we shall be committed to it from the start.

Mr. Wilson's diplomacy in the first instance stressed the illegality of Germany's submarine campaign. Germany desisted for a time, only to resume the attack and bring the United States into the war. All but a few Americans thought when war was declared that our contribution would consist of little more than our navy and our money. They learned differently.

Mr. Roosevelt seems to hope that the mere threat of a boycott will bring the aggressor nations to their senses. It may. Again it may not. Japan is substantially self-sufficient so far as food is concerned. Japan will not easily be beaten to her knees, and the threat of a boycott may only serve to inflame the patriotic ardor of the Japanese.

If the boycott is adopted and it doesn't work; if, while it is in progress, Japan's conquests continue, then what will Mr. Roosevelt do? The moment came when Mr. Wilson found himself with no alternative but war. Does not Mr. Roosevelt's policy invite the coming of the day when he, too, may have no alternative but resort to arms? It would be difficult today to obtain a declaration of war from congress, but after months of propaganda the task may be simplified. It was so in 1917; it may be so again in 1938.

Once more America is found actively on England's side in international policy. As before, America can expect no material gain which can compensate for the risk Mr. Roosevelt invites us to take. Our participation this time is not to make the world safe for democracy, but to uphold the sanctity of treaties. In fact, Britain, with an enormously larger stake in China than ours, is to have our help in preserving her imperial interests in China. With our help the English cotton and wool trade is to recover the markets won by Japan, which happens incidentally to be a far better customer of ours than of England's.

It is quite natural that Mr. Roosevelt is bringing the Wilson foreign policy back to life. He believed in it in 1917 when he was Mr. Wilson's assistant secretary of the navy. He indorsed the league of nations when he was a candidate for the vice presidency in the 1920 campaign. He was a grown man then and grown men's fundamental opinions undergo little change. The same theorizing which impelled him to favor entangling America in foreign quarrels a score of years ago is at work again.

At the dedication of the new bridge Mr. Roosevelt repeated his declaration that he hates war. He repeated his determination to avoid it. The crowd applauded. He was expressing their inmost desire. The crowd also applauded Mr. Wilson when he campaigned on the slogan "He kept us out of war." They accepted his word and did not examine the meaning of his diplomatic acts. A month after his inauguration America was in the war.

THE WAR THE WORLD FEARED

September 2, 1939

The beginning of another war invites a forecast of the state of Europe at its conclusion. Compare these expectations with those expressed in "The Twilight of the Kings," on Aug. 2, 1914.

The morning headlines told the story the world has dreaded to read. Europe's war is on. Hitler answered the question whether he would take the one step which would be fatal. Would he go over the brink? He has and Europe now is confronted with the event which many of its wise men said it could not survive.

Europe will survive. Its germ of life has resisted its history and its history has been a record of great wars growing in intensity of passion, employing increasing millions of men and weapons of increasing destructiveness. Physically the survivors will be alive. Culturally and intellectually they will have preserved their heritages. But that will not tell the story.

When this misery has run its course there will be new battle mementos on old battlefields long familiar to European armies. There will be new hospitals filled with new victims permanently maimed. The earthly scars will slowly be smoothed out. The grass will be planted, much of it on new graves. Masons and carpenters will repair buildings and a new generation will be started. This much we are vouchsafed by experience and history.

From the memories of the world war we can derive certain other anticipations and previews. Some of the peoples, whether victorious or defeated, will be reduced to despair. Politically they may be exposed to savage revolutions following a destructive peace. Their economy will be broken down, their productive institutions ruined. They will be the prey of melancholy and want. Their wounds will not heal quickly and they will recover but slowly under the depressing influences of skepticism regarding human sanity and doubt of an ultimate good.

What will emerge as dominant we cannot know. Hitler has released more than the forces which prevail in war. He has released also forces which must be reckoned with when the better armies have imposed the will of some nations upon others and have determined who is master and who is servant. Hitler may have pronounced the death of the totalitarian states. He may have pronounced the death of two great empires and the subjugation of Europe to the rule of the Nazis. He may have ushered in the Red revolution. He may have pronounced the extinction of European bourgeois society and the death of a social order.

The survivors will be prostrated with debts which cannot be paid. Their available wealth will be destroyed. Some peoples may go under the yoke. Their masters may themselves be brutalized by the conditions they impose upon the people they defeat. We cannot refuse any of these thoughts. Their ferocious brutalities are sustained by the picture of Russia from 1918 until now, by the post-war experiences of starving Germany and its civil wars, of Italy succumbing to Fascism, and of the smaller nations struggling between Red and black dictatorship. Europe has every reason to fear the peace as much as it fears the war.

Could it have been avoided? One answer was contained in the prophetic cartoon published by the London Herald twenty years ago, when the Versailles treaty was signed, in which Clemenceau, leaving the council room, stopped to remark: "Strange, but I thought I heard a child crying." Hidden from the peacemaker's view by a pillar was the class of 1940. It is useless at this time to review the intents and the conse-

quences of that peace. The time to revert to this subject will come when other peacemakers seek to impose another peace upon countries they have brought to submission. If there are admonitions, that will be the time to call them back to life.

Hitler's statement of the immediate cause might have seemed reasonable and convincing, but the world has a poor opinion of his good faith. His voice has echoes in Austria and in Czecho-Slovakia. It has an echo in Russia. The echo accuses him of perfidy which he justifies as a means to an end. Perfidy is not a strange element in international relations. Hitler, however, has too much rejoiced in it. "Munich" is a word new within the last year in diplomatic language. Hitler has given it the significance and meaning it has. It spells betrayal.

Another Germany, governed by less brutal men, might have presented a good cause to world opinion and have had the weight of that opinion on its side. But the Germany which made the demands is the Germany which persecuted the Jews, oppressed people because of race and religion, denied them the free exercise of their beliefs in their cathedrals, churches, and synagogues, imprisoned their priests, ministers, and rabbis, denied freedom of opinion and expression, made the purge and the concentration camp instruments of domestic policy, glorified force and might, and ridiculed liberty. These vices obscure the faults and errors of the opposition. They give Germany's enemies the glamor of a crusade against evil, against oppression, and tyranny.

122

The American people have sympathy for all the other peoples who must suffer if this war spreads as it seems inevitably destined to do. The sympathy may be involved in a great deal of emotionalism against which a caution should be uttered. Twenty-five years ago in August a terrible war was raging because imperialistic programs had clashed in a corner of Europe. As that war progressed its hideousness produced a hope, nowhere stronger than in the United States, that it might be a war to end war, to make people free, and to give them hope. With that illusion America entered the conflict. How can we have the illusion again?

THE NOMINATION

July 19, 1940

The nomination of Mr. Roosevelt for a third term provides the occasion for a glance backward and a warning of what is to come.

For the first time in the history of the United States, and at the most dangerous time in which it could be done, an American party has renominated a man for a third consecutive term in the presidency.

This man, in his second term, undertook to make the Supreme court a ratifying board for his decrees. In his first term he had been accustomed to issue executive orders which he expected congress to enact into laws by acclaim and without study or discussion. He expected that such a congress would ratify his decree destroying the federal judiciary as a separate branch of government. He demanded that the senators and representatives, without dissent or opposition, give him a Supreme court of yesmen who would approve any law he issued.

He expected obedience because he had already reduced the national legislature to acceptance of bills as written. If, in his second term, he could have enforced his will, the government of the United States would have consisted in reality of the chief executive and no other independent branch of government. Congress and the court would have disappeared.

When congress, to his astonishment, defeated him in his purpose, he resolved that his supremacy should be reestablished by the ejection of the congressional rebels who had opposed him. He undertook his great purge and failed again. His idea of government was revealed in his second term. Now he is the man to whom the Democratic convention has submitted and for whom it has broken the rule which has kept the presidency from being available to the ambitions of any willful man who wanted prolonged tenure.

The convention did this for this willful man at a time when people in many lands are losing their freedom and being governed as disfranchised subjects of autocratic power, without the vote, without representative assemblies, and without independent judges.

The party which has presented the nation with this shameless historic episode is the party which says that the military forces of oppression are preparing to descend on these shores. It is the war party

123

which has supported in Washington a policy of intervention in world conflict to save democracy in other lands.

The party which has broken down the American safeguard against dictatorship has nominated a man who for seven years has been trying to dictate and who for three years has been preparing his country for war in Europe and in Asia. In a false plank in its platform the party which nominated the war-maker declared for peace. The falseness of that declaration was revealed a few hours after it was made by the nomination of a man who seeks war, has done everything in his power to incite it, and whose record in the White House is a record of campaign and platform pledges ignored and violated. He alone could tell the country to what degree, by his commitments to France and Great Britain, he is himself responsible for the outbreak of war in September, and how soon after election America will be drawn into the conflict if he wins.

From what is known of his acts and utterances and of the acts and utterances of his ambassadors to Great Britain, France, and Poland the responsibility seems to be very grave. The Democratic convention has nominated for a third term a man who almost established a dictatorship in his second, and who has already prepared his plan for the conscription of the American people, their resources, and their enterprises, not only in event of war, but when war is imminent.

There were some voices raised against this in the convention, but they were feeble against the roar of the purse-controlled elements of the party and the voice of the mob which had been planted in the hall to drown any protest which might be made. The party, no doubt, has men in it who perceive this event with dismay, who, as citizens, regret not only that any man given power by their party should abuse it, who regret that the national purse should have been used to the disgrace of the party and the peril of the nation. They could not, however, find the spirit or the voice to rebuke the action fittingly. Senator Carter Glass, in spite of infirmities, tried to make his protest, but the man who wanted the nomination had too well prepared the way for it.

As the convention adjourns after its great disservice to the republic the honest public feeling is one of dismay and disgust. The responsible members will bear the reproach of their actions to the end of their days.

WE GET THE BASES

September 4, 1940

Since this editorial was published, THE TRIBUNE *has frequently urged the State department to complete the work by persuading the British, Dutch, and French to grant independence to their remaining possessions in the Americas.*

President Roosevelt notified congress yesterday of the agreement between the United States and Great Britain which gives this country leases for naval and air bases in British-American possessions.

Lord Lothian, British ambassador,

in a note to the state department, said the leases would apply to the eastern side of the Bahamas, the southern coast of Jamaica, the west coast of St. Lucia, the west coast of Trinidad in the Gulf of Paria, to the island of Antigua, and to British Guiana within 50 miles of Georgetown.

THE TRIBUNE rejoices to make this announcement, which fulfills a policy advocated by this newspaper since 1922. In spite of much discouragement, THE TRIBUNE persisted, month by month and year by year, in calling for these additions to the national defense. It may be found, as we think it will be, that this is the greatest contribution of this newspaper to the country's history since the nomination of Lincoln.

The agreement is not in the terms THE TRIBUNE would have preferred. Nevertheless, any arrangement which gives the United States naval and air bases in regions which must be brought within the American defense zone is to be accepted as a triumph.

THE ALLIANCE AGAINST AMERICA

September 28, 1940

Japan joins the Berlin-Rome Axis.

Japan has now joined in a treaty with Germany and Italy directed against the United States. The three powers have agreed that if the United States enters the war in Europe on the side of England or the war in Asia on the side of China, all three powers will make war on the United States.

This was Japan's answer to the embargo placed by Mr. Roosevelt on the export of scrap steel to Japan and the answer of Germany and Italy to our departures from strict neutrality in the European conflict. Perhaps some Americans were astonished by the announcement from Berlin, but they must have been naive, indeed.

Surely Mr. Roosevelt was not astonished, and, equally surely, he is not displeased by the latest turn of events. His diplomacy resulted precisely as George Washington and every other sensible man in our nation's history said it would. Because we have taken sides in old-world quarrels, we have acquired old-world enemies. For the first time in our history a foreign alliance against us has been perfected. When and if it suits their purpose to do so, they will make war on us. So far as pretexts for war are concerned, they have them already.

Mr. Roosevelt now has the critical international situation which, in his reckoning, his third term candidacy requires. He has it because he made it. Logically, his position today corresponds closely to that of the man who poisoned his mother and father and then pleaded for mercy on the ground that he was an orphan. Mr. Roosevelt is pleading for votes in the November election on the ground that the nation is faced with an emergency. He made the emergency.

There is no need here to examine the question whether Mr. Roosevelt should have embargoed the sale of scrap to Japan. The significant fact is that Mr. Roosevelt waited until the last week of September, 1940, to issue his decree. Every moral and legal justification for his action existed as well two years ago as now, five weeks before the third term election. Mr. Roosevelt wanted the crisis when he wanted it and not before.

That is why the United States today finds itself the enemy of three great military powers so situated that they may be able to bring war upon us on two flanks simultaneously. That is why the people of the United States today face a future beset with troubles which might have been avoided.

If we are lucky enough to escape war, despite Mr. Roosevelt, we may still have to devote a needlessly large share of our productive resources to maintaining a military establishment of stupendous size. Conscription may become a permanent institution in American life, along with armament expenditures on an unprecedented scale.

If war is the consequence, it is not likely to be one war. Twenty years after Germany was prostrate she had developed the most powerful military machine the world ever saw, and was again on the march. If we prevent Japan from taking Indo-China from the French, the East Indies from the Dutch, etc., we have solved no problems. We have only assumed a responsibility for the future of those territories. We don't want them, and whoever has them, whether native governments or some one else, will hold them, thanks to our power to maintain the status quo which we shall have created. That means a continuing

liability. It means that we must, at any moment, be ready to defend these places, 6,000 miles and more from our shores, against any nation or combination of nations which may covet them.

The acceptance of such a responsibility means that the America which we have known is dead. From being a nation which habitually minded its own business in its own sphere, we shall have become a great imperial power, set upon a course of foreign conquest and domination, a ruler of remote lands and alien races. The costs of maintaining such a policy will be stupendous and not the least of them will be the loss of our democratic faith. A democracy cannot rule subject peoples and remain a democracy.

———

IF RUSSIA WINS

July 30, 1941

The friendship of Hitler and Stalin was cemented in the Russo-German agreements of August, 1939. Two years later, on June 22, when Hitler had defeated all his enemies on the continent, he turned against Russia. Another speedy victory by the Nazis was widely expected. The Editor here suggests that the Russian resistance may prove successful and looks ahead to the time when the Red army may march westward into Europe. The editorial is interesting not only for its accurate forecast but also as evidence of THE TRIBUNE'S *refusal from the start to accept Stalin in the role of liberator. The myth of a beneficent bolshevism obtained the widest credence, thanks to the persistent efforts of the Office of War Information in*

America and the Ministry of Information in Britain. Only now, six years later, has the soundness of the views expressed here received general acceptance.

The world's largest armies are engaged in battle to determine which of two hateful systems of government shall survive. Each system is remorseless and powerful. That they could exist at all is something that does not get its explanation from economist, from historian, or even from the psychologist. That the mastery of Europe is the prize for which they fight is a dreadful testimony to the character and the potentialities of what was called the world's greatest civilization.

These two systems are created of fury and error, supported by scientific knowledge, devilish ingenuity, and the highest degree of technological skill and far-seeing calculation. The modern barbarian has retained all the primitive savage traits and to them he has added the dehumanized mind of the greatest scientists and even of the scholars. All the progress of the human race has been made the servant of its basest desires. The spectacle is appalling.

For the first time since the German machine went to war it has encountered another which it could not immediately overwhelm. The Nazis have had successes which would have been decisive in any other European scene of action. They have driven far and hard and have won victories. They have crossed the territories occupied by Russia at the beginning of the war in agreement with Hitler and they are striking at the principal cities of Russia. But they are not yet within sight of a decision. Apparently, the Russian Army is unshattered. It is fighting with good morale and also with skill.

German commentators are preparing the German public not to expect a quick finish. Russia is vast, its man power is tremendous, and its equipment seems to be holding up. Its armies are familiar with the German tactics. Movements which dumfounded Germany's foes in other stages of the war do not terrify the Russians into submission and surrender. Superior striking power remains in the hands of the Germans. They have a dominance but it cannot be called mastery. They haven't suffered what could be called a defeat nor have they gained a conclusive victory.

A war of uncertain outcome is waged in battles which are beginning to take a heavy toll not only of the Russians but of the Germans. A sudden collapse of the Russian resistance is not out of question, but it must be regarded as without evidence at the present time. It can as well be a long war as a short one.

The British government and its associate, the American government, are now on the Russian side. Mr. Churchill must be taking such consolation as he can from the axiom of statecraft when it doesn't know what to do, that you don't have to cross a bridge until you come to it. For immediate purposes he must hope that the Russians win. He must also know that if they do he will be out of one terrible problem and in another which he could hardly bear to contemplate.

If Hitler's military power met its death in Russia, Churchill would be relieved of trouble number one. Subject Europe would rise again, badly shaken and shattered by its experiences, but reemerging. But what of the victorious Russian army, recrossing the land which the Nazis had taken and coming west with the hammer and sickle, the dictatorship of the proletariat, the class war, and the liquidation of the bourgeoisie? Where would Mr. Churchill stop that?

Does any one suppose that a victorious Stalin would listen to the advice or remonstrances of the man who hadn't been able to put an expeditionary force in Europe when the Reds were fighting for their lives against an invader who had sworn to destroy them? Where would Stalin stop? Would another war begin with British and American troops trying to stem forces they had supported?

No outcome in this war in the east can be viewed without dismay except one in which the two hateful systems destroyed each other. If both were wrecked inside Russia, European civilization might observe the miracle which had rescued it. Everywhere in Europe there are communist remnants of the great attempt at world revolution which followed the other war. They were once a powerful party in Germany and their underground cells remain there. Hitler hasn't killed them all nor has he all of them in concentration camps.

French communists were strong enough to wreck France with the Popular Front government, and altho they are underground they are still there. Franco did his best, but he hasn't killed all the communists in Spain. A victorious Stalin would invite them all to rise. Their doctrine of the class war is a doctrine of uncompromising hatred, hatred not only of the great private enterprisers but of the entire middle class. Liquidation means the physical destruction of everything that stands in their way, and their experiences in recent years when they themselves were being liquidated have added to their ferocity.

No one should indulge in any dreamy speculation of the deliverance of Europe under the protection of the great liberal powers if Stalin is the controler of new forces dominating the continent. His perfidies equal Hitler's and his ruthlessness is not less. The communist recognizes in Great Britain and the United States, two enemies, different in type from the Nazi foe, but fully as hostile and less akin to him in thought and purpose than his German neighbor. The present war is one between forces of similar purposes and some common ideas. The next war would be between the bitterest of enemies, and if the Russians were in the ascendancy it would be a war without quarter.

Mr. Churchill knows this, if Mr. Roosevelt doesn't. The Red ally of today might be the Red terror of tomorrow. If that is not to be the event, then Hitler continues to be the terror unless both tyrannies find a common grave in the war brought on by their own treachery to every one with whom they have dealt, including themselves.

WHAT HAS ROOSEVELT PROMISED CHURCHILL?

August 15, 1941

The Atlantic conference took place off Argentia, Newfoundland, from Aug. 9 to 12, 1941. The world learned of it on Aug. 14.

Mr. Roosevelt's dangerous ambition always to do what no other President ever did and to be the man who shakes the world led him to meet Mr. Churchill, as is now disclosed, at sea. There, he, the head of a nation which is not at war, and the head of the British empire, which is at war, signed their names to an eight point war and peace program as if both countries not only were fighting side by side but saw their way to victory. Mr. Roosevelt undoubtedly was at sea but Mr. Churchill, altho on the British battleship Prince of Wales or the United States cruiser Augusta with Mr. Roosevelt, was never out of the back room.

The British prime minister must have snapped at the chance to join in this meeting with Mr. Roosevelt, which would so appeal to the theatricality of the latter, with its furtiveness, its preliminary rumors, and all its window dressing. It was, of course, imitative and ominously so. It suggested Hitler and Mussolini, under the cover of censorship, meeting at Brenner pass before they undertook some new stroke.

For Mr. Churchill the event would be, he could hope, that last step which would bring him what he has awaited as his salvation—the final delivery on Mr. Roosevelt's commitments, the delivery of the United States with all its man power into the war at all points. Mr. Churchill would appreciate that Mr. Roosevelt in the eyes of the world became his full ally. The Englishman could believe that everything extraordinary in the occurrence would compromise the United States beyond redemption and give Britain the full reward for its patient and skillful manipulation of a great country against that country's interests and against the will of its people.

Mr. Roosevelt himself had that end in view. As head of a nation at peace he had no right to discuss war aims with the ruler of a country at war. He had no right to take a chair at such a conference. He had no regard for his constitutional duties or his oath of office when he did so. He not only likes to shatter traditions, he likes to shatter the checks and restraints which were put on his office. He is thoroly un-American. His ancestry is constantly emerging. He is the true descendant of that James Roosevelt, his great-grandfather who was a Tory in New York during the Revolution and took the oath of allegiance to the British king.

He is the true representative of the southern connection of the family which would have destroyed the Union, of James Bulloch, the Confederate agent who in London equipped the commerce destroyers. He comes of a stock that has never fought for the country and he now betrays it altho it has repudiated his program and him with it.

The document Mr. Roosevelt and Mr. Churchill signed is not a revelation of what the two had to say to each other. They didn't have to put

129

on this big show with its well arranged provocative secrecy merely to discuss those pretentious but meaningless eight points for the reconstruction of a peaceful world. That interchange didn't require any meeting of the minds out at sea. Mr. Churchill wouldn't have felt justified in making a lunch date merely to talk over a bit of rhetoric.

The Englishman was not interested in words about peaceful traverse of the seas, self-determination, the common enjoyment of trade, the equitable use of raw materials, social security, and the abandonment of the use of force. His business is to preserve Britain, preserve the British empire and its dominant position in the world, and to knock off Hitler.

As the fighting prime minister he has not shown any interest in declarations of war aims or peace terms. His disposition has been to repress discussion of them in parliament as if he regarded them as mere distractions and of no importance. His job is to win the war, if he can, and he has been told by his generals that he will need all the American soldiers he can get. Without them he was not able to take advantage of Germany's war with Russia. He wants soldiers.

Churchill could humor Mr. Roosevelt and treat his grandiloquence and moral excursions with the patience required to get something important out of a talkative man. The American people can rest assured that Mr. Churchill was paying little attention to the rehash of the Wilsonian futilities, to the freedom of the seas and the freedom of peoples, such as the people of India, for instance. What he wanted to know of Mr. Roosevelt was: When are you coming across? And it is the answer to that question that concerns the American people who have voted 4 to 1 that they are not going across at all unless their government drags them in against their will.

One phrase in the statement would have Mr. Churchill's complete approval—"after final destruction of the Nazi tyranny." To that he committed the President of the United States in circumstances as spectacular and theatrical as could be arranged. Mr. Roosevelt pledged himself to the destruction of Hitler and the Nazis. In the circumstances in which this was done Mr. Churchill would insist that it was the pledge of a government, binding upon the country. The country repudiates it. Mr. Roosevelt had no authority and can find none for making such a pledge. He was more than outside the country. He was outside his office. The spectacle was one of two autocratic rulers, one of them determining the destiny of his country in the matter of war or peace absolutely in his own will, as if his subjects were without voice.

The country rejects that idea of its government.

———

WE ALL HAVE ONLY ONE TASK

December 8, 1941

The destruction of the fleet at Pearl Harbor on Dec. 7, 1941, stunned the American people. This editorial, published on Page One, helped to restore

130

confidence as was made clear in many grateful letters and telephone calls. The judgments expressed here regarding responsibility for the disaster had later to be modified as facts which had been carefully concealed from the public came to light.

War has been forced on America by an insane clique of Japanese militarists who apparently see the desperate conflict into which they have led their country as the only thing that can prolong their power.

Thus the thing that we all feared, that so many of us have worked with all our hearts to avert, has happened. That is all that counts. It has happened. America faces war thru no volition of any American.

Recriminations are useless and we doubt that they will be indulged in. Certainly not by us. All that matters today is that we are in the war and the nation must face that simple fact. All of us, from this day forth, have only one task. That is to strike with all our might to protect and preserve the American freedom that we all hold dear.

THE PHILIPPINE WAR

December 27, 1941

THE TRIBUNE *persisted in emphasizing the war against Japan during the long months when the official propaganda was seeking to concentrate all interest on the European war. In this editorial, published three weeks after Pearl Harbor, an amphibious war in which airplane carriers would be the capital ships was foreshadowed.*

The lack of modern weapons in the Philippines is only one of the explanations for the inability of our forces to prevent the Japanese landings. We lack numbers, also. Even if our army had all the planes, tanks, and up-to-date shooting irons that could be used, there would still be too few soldiers available to guard all the threatened points.

Islands, it used to be said, can be taken by whatever power controls the sea. That theorem of war still holds true if recognition is given to the fact that control of the sea is possible only where control of the air is maintained. When England's navy was all-powerful, Britain demonstrated on many occasions that she could take any island she wanted. The Japanese used their sea power—reinforced by air power—to take Wake Island the other day. They can hold it until they lose control of the sea and air in the Wake region.

So far as the Philippines are concerned, the best strategical minds in our army have long recognized the extraordinary difficulty of defending these outposts, located as they are in waters which the Japanese fleet and air force dominate. The army was inclined to regard the Philippines as a liability and was not displeased at the decision to grant the Filipinos their independence.

There were, and perhaps still are, two schools of thought in the navy. One recognized the great difficulty of fighting a major naval battle on the other side of the Pacific and accordingly agreed with the army's judgment. The other school, placed in command by the present administration, believed our battle fleet could best the Japanese navy in its own waters. Many of our admirals have publicly indorsed this view. Only two months ago, for example, Rear Adm. Bemis, commandant of the 16th naval district in the Philippines, returned to San Francisco to say that "we in the Philippines are just waiting for the whistle to blow. We are all ready."

That was the view of the dominant faction of the navy. It becomes plainer every day that the judgment was ill-founded. The Japanese succeeded in doing great damage to our fleet in Pearl Harbor. It is reasonable to assume that the enemy's planes could have done even greater damage had our fleet approached the western side of the Pacific where it could have been attacked by land-based planes as well as carrier planes. The Japanese understood the principles of modern war. We have had to learn them the hard way.

Even if we lose the Philippines, we shall not lose the war. With an overwhelming air force, based on ships, we can move progressively across the Pacific. We can build planes much faster than the Japanese can and we have fast merchant ships which can readily be converted into airplane carriers. We can advance from island to island as on stepping stones. We shall have to acquire skill in landing operations but with time the job can be accomplished. It will take a great deal longer if the stonehead school which didn't believe in the power of the air arm and is responsible for the Pearl Harbor defeat regains the control.

GEN. MacARTHUR

January 28, 1942

One of the curiosities of the war wa.; the persistent effort, particularly in the left wing press, to belittle Gen. MacArthur. Perhaps the purpose was to discourage the sending to him of supplies and reenforcements which otherwise would go to Russia or be used on the second front in Europe which Russia desired.

THE TRIBUNE was never in doubt about Gen. MacArthur's outstanding qualities, as this editorial attests, and thruout the war led in demanding that adequate means be sent him. He has enjoyed the same measure of support since the occupation of Japan. THE TRIBUNE has often called attention to the contrast between the success of his policies of moderation and the failure of the policies of revenge pursued in the defeated countries of Europe.

Gen. MacArthur succeeded in only a few years in making not only first class soldiers but more particularly a first class army in the Philippines. Obviously he has confidence in the Filipinos and they in him. Gen. MacArthur is one of the relatively few military leaders in recent history who has been able to forge an efficient fighting machine, strong in attack and alert in defense, from so-called native material. That speaks well for the Filipinos and for the qualities of leadership possessed by the general. He has the kind of dynamic personality which inspires courage, resolution, and initiative in his officers and men.

Gen. MacArthur has always been

a leader. He was top man in his class at West Point. He was first captain of the cadet corps and his subsequent career in the army shows that the honor was a just recognition of character and competence. Stories about his personal courage are almost numberless and almost all of them are true. It is a fact, for example, that contrary to custom and even to orders he personally participated in trench raids in the last war.

In this war Gen. MacArthur has again shown that he is not only a man of courage with the gift of leadership but also a strategist of the first quality. Thus far he appears to be alone among the generals on our side to have demonstrated any real ability. The conduct of the campaign in Luzon indicates that he knew from the start what was to be expected of the enemy and how to counter it most effectively. He seems to have foreseen clearly the character of modern warfare. He did not make the mistake of attempting with insufficient forces to defend Manila. He swung his army into a position which could be held with the strength at his disposal, but he has not been content to let the initiative pass to the enemy. His defense of his weakened left flank by attacking on the right was a brilliant maneuver of which any of the great captains might have been proud.

Tho Gen. MacArthur's army is outnumbered, it is safe to predict that he will hold on as long as he has ammunition to fire. The Japanese, however, have control of the air and the sea in the vicinity of Luzon and are able to receive a steady flow of reënforcements and supplies, while denying them to our army. For the long pull the chances of a successful defense of the Philippines are therefore anything but bright.

Whether Gen. MacArthur would obey an order to leave his men is a question to which he alone holds the answer, but certainly our government should make every effort to withdraw him if the position of his army becomes desperate, as it well may. Our side has need of him. We cannot afford to let him be killed or captured. On the record of this war to date, he is the one general who has shown himself fit for the position of commander in chief of the united nations.

––––

INVOLUNTARY SERVITUDE
March 5, 1943

The New Deal administration kept up the agitation for a labor draft until the war ended. THE TRIBUNE *opposed the plan from the start and called all such measures slave bills. Other editorials published at this period emphasized that America's war industries were vastly more productive than those of any other country, ally or enemy, all of which had instituted forced labor in one form or another.*

It doesn't take an expert on the Constitution to see that the proposed draft of civilian man power for assignment at the President's discretion to industry or agriculture can't live alongside the 13th amendment. That amendment very clearly states: "Neither slavery nor involuntary servitude, except as a punishment for crime whereof the party shall have been duly convicted, shall exist within the United States, or any place subject to their jurisdiction."

When somebody proposes flatly to tell any woman between 18 and 50 and any man between 18 and 64 what kind of job he shall take, where he must work, and what hours, pay, or other conditions he must accept, it is difficult to discover what other words than "involuntary servitude" will accurately describe the citizen's status. Yet this bill was drafted by a lawyer, Mr. Grenville Clark. It was introduced in the senate by a lawyer, Mr. Warren Austin. It has been supported by the secretary of war, Mr. Stimson, who is a lawyer as well as a close friend of Mr. Clark. And it evidently has the approval of the President, who holds a law degree.

It is impossible that these lawyers, or any lawyers, or, indeed, any one at all familiar with the Constitution, should be ignorant of the fact that the proposed legislation contravenes the 13th amendment. There are only a few circumstances in which the government can use compulsion to exact the citizen's services. It can coerce him to defend his country, and it can coerce him to enforce his country's laws. A citizen can be conscripted for military service in war, and in peace a sheriff can deputize any citizen. But nowhere in our law or custom is there any precedent for requiring the citizen in his capacity as wage earner to place himself at the disposal of the state.

When the Constitution granted congress power to provide for organizing, arming, disciplining, governing, and calling forth the militia, it was taken for granted that the citizen owed it to his country to bear arms in its defense. The 2d amendment further clarified the citizen's military obligations when it gave him the right to keep and bear arms because "a well regulated militia" is "necessary to the security of a free state" and arms are necessary to the militia. Finally, by an act of 1903, the militia was specifically defined. It consists of every able bodied male citizen and every able bodied male of foreign birth who has declared his intention to become a citizen, who is more than 18 and less than 45. The organized militia is to be known as the National Guard and the remainder as the reserve militia. Thus it was understood that all citizens of proper age, even if not on regular militia duty, were still subject at all times to call. Conscription acts are, therefore, merely a convenience in summoning inactive militia to military service.

Nobody can pretend, however, that because able bodied males are required to give military service if necessary to their country, there is the slightest constitutional justification for assuming that all citizens, both men and women, can be required to place themselves at the disposal of the government as civilians. Conscription is an extraordinary power of government, to be invoked only in the event of invasion, threat of invasion, or rebellion. The service commanded is military and nothing else.

To attempt to torture this into sanction for the government to levy upon the civil talents of the citizen, or to teach him new ones, is clearly to invade the freedom of the person specifically guaranteed by the 13th amendment. Congress will be well advised to reject any arguments that the administration may advance that national security demands the passage of this bill. We cannot secure the safety of our country by stripping the citizens who compose it of their constitutional protections.

STATES ACROSS THE SEA

April 25, 1943

This editorial, prompted by the propaganda for American membership in a federal union of nations, attracted the widest attention thruout the English-speaking world.

The people who are demanding that the United States yield its sovereignty to some kind of international organization seem to be more eager to stir up a row in this country than to achieve closer international cooperation. Certainly it is difficult to see why those who say their goal is integration of the free peoples have consistently neglected the most obvious method of achieving it, and the one that would be most readily acceptable to the American people.

The method is found in the Constitution of the United States. The provisions of Article IV. are not at all onerous. Section 3 says that "new states may be admitted by the congress into this Union." A joint resolution is all that is required. The qualification that when new states are created existing states shall not be deprived of territory or merged without their consent is obviously no bar to the admission of overseas members of an enlarged Union. Section 4 says "the United States shall guarantee to every state in this Union a republican form of government" and goes on to pledge the central government to protect the new states from invasion and, upon request, from domestic violence.

That's all there is to it. If the British commonwealth and the nations of western Europe wish to enjoy closer association with us in foreign policy, defense, trade, currency, patents, and all the other fields of federal jurisdiction, and if for our part we wish similarly to link ourselves to them, the way to accomplish the result is clear. All they need do is adopt written constitutions and apply for membership and all we need do is accept them as we once accepted Texas.

This method is obviously in accord with the provisions of our Constitution. All the schemes proposed by the international set are repugnant to it. Plainly, these people are as unfamiliar with as they are uninterested in the document that Mr. Gladstone described in the often quoted phrase as "the most wonderful work ever struck off at a given time by the brain and purpose of man." They think they can skip around it or over it. In fact, the Constitution, as Mr. Gladstone realized, is a stern document, with living force, and it cannot be perverted to the detriment of the American people by a handful of noisy lobbyists.

Great Britain could come into the Union, for example, as four states, England, Scotland, Wales, and Ireland. Canada could constitute another state. Australia, New Zealand, and the contiguous islands might form still another. [This last should be a particularly easy transition because Australia is now aware of the inability of the British empire to furnish protection and of our ability—and willingness—to do so. Practically speaking, Australia is out of the empire today as all but the most literal minded know.] South Africa presents a much more difficult problem. The laws of this dominion violate the 13th, 14th and 15th amendments, and there is little reason to believe that the dominion is prepared to accept our views of human freedom.

For the people of Britain, particularly, statehood would have many advantages. American man power, industry, and wealth would be instantly and automatically available if British territory were threatened with invasion. Inclusion within our tariff boundaries should prove a stimulant to British industry. Our gold reserve offers another attraction. Membership in our Union would give the British an opportunity to rid themselves, once and for all, of the incubus of their nobility and the aristocratic system that goes with it. Britain would have to give up its king, but as his constitutional powers are said to be merely nominal or, in any event, are not exercised, the change to a republican form of government could be made without difficulty.

Certainly the handkissers and Tories in this country should welcome the closer relationship if only because it would strengthen their representation in congress. They should look forward pleasurably to more intimate social and political ties with their English friends, particularly as the new relationship would be that of equals, living within the same political system.

A federal republic made up of English speaking states on both sides of the Atlantic and Pacific would be strong enough to dispense with allies, but if it desired to do so, the more advanced states of western Europe that show aptitude for constitutional government might also be included.

So far as the United States and the British commonwealth are concerned, the easiest and most direct means of achieving joint action in defense, foreign affairs, and economic policy is the one described in our Constitution. The failure to consider this time tested plan throws grave doubt upon the sincerity of those who are advocating alternative and untried arrangements.

The United States today is by all odds the strongest nation in the world, and its system of government is at once the freest and the most stable among the great nations. The people admitted to our Union will enjoy as we do the inestimable advantage of a written constitution containing a bill of rights, as the fundamental law. Their liberties will be guaranteed them by the federal Constitution and all the power possessed by the federal government will stand behind the pledge. They can have every advantage that any of the schemes of world organization have offered and none of the disadvantages.

136

THE NAZI TRIALS

July 24, 1945

THE TRIBUNE *was one of the few newspapers in America or abroad to challenge the legality of the Nuernberg and Tokyo trials.*

A re-reading of Mr. Justice Jackson's report to the President on the forthcoming trials of the German war criminals before an improvised international tribunal arouses many misgivings.

We can see no possible objection to trying the Nazi leaders and others responsible for German crimes in established courts for violating national laws which were in existence at the time the offenses occurred. If this simple rule were followed, none of the guilty would escape the hangman. The Jackson plan to achieve the same end calls for ex post facto proceedings, in courts recruited for the purpose.

Mr. Justice Jackson has evolved the theory that the law the Nazis violated is the Kellogg-Briand outlawry of war pact, but he does not deny that this treaty carried no penalties and set up no court for trying offenders. The proper use of the pact is to establish the fact that Germany's invasions of neighboring countries were illegal, for that is what the treaty plainly said. If the invasions were unlawful, it follows that every Pole, Frenchman, Czech, or Norwegian who died in the fighting or before a firing squad was the victim of murder, under Polish, French, Czech, or Norwegian law, and his murderers can be punished accordingly in the courts of those countries.

What Nazi leader could escape punishment under this theory? Not Goering, surely, for he helped plan the invasions, or any of his fellows in the top ranks of the party, or the gauleiters or any of the others whom Mr. Jackson means to bring to justice under his ex post facto scheme. Why, then, resort to a plan which offends the sense of justice and sets a precedent for some day dragging Americans before foreign judges for trial under ex post facto laws?

Moreover, the Jackson plan drips with hypocrisy. Probably few Americans as yet fully realize how grossly illegal was the conduct of our own administration in the months before Pearl Harbor. Our army and navy, taking orders from our President, violated the rules laid down for neutrals. We used our armed forces in violation of our obligations under treaties. We were engaged in a shooting war in 1941 without a declaration of war by congress and without having suffered any direct injury of the sort which is supposed to justify a declaration of war.

The hypocrisy of some of our allies is easier for Americans to see. Here, for example, is a paragraph from Mr. Justice Jackson's indictment:

"Our people were outraged by the oppressions, the cruelest forms of torture, the large-scale murder, and the wholesale confiscation of property which initiated the Nazi regime within Germany. They witnessed persecution of the greatest enormity on religious, political, and racial grounds, the breakdown of trade unions, and the liquidation of all religious and moral influences."

Read "Bolshevik" for "Nazi" and "Russia" for "Germany" and the passage makes equally good sense. A Bolshevik judge who would convict a Nazi under such an indictment would deserve to be remembered until the end of time as an arch hypocrite among arch hypocrites.

Mr. Jackson goes on: "This was not the legitimate activity of a state within its own boundaries but was preparatory to the launching of an international course of aggression and war, with the evil intention, openly expressed by the Nazis, of capturing the form of the German state as an instrumentality for spreading their rule to other countries."

Again make the substitution of "Bolshevik" for "Nazi" and "Russian" for "German" and the indictment is equally sound. The charge so amended can be documented a thousand times over from the writings of Lenin and Stalin, the proceedings of the Third International, and the historical record of what has happened to Finland, Poland, and a lot of other countries overrun by Russia.

It is, perhaps, unnecessary to add that the English jurists summoned to sit in judgment will be chosen by a government whose predecessors recognized the Nazi gang as the lawful rulers of Germany, dealt with them, and assented to many of their most offensive acts.

There is no need to resort to blatant hypocrisy to convict the Nazi criminals. There is no need to improvise ex post facto laws and kangaroo courts. The right way to dis-

pose of the Nazis is to try them under existing laws in existing national courts. No guilty man will escape.

THE FUTURE
August 14, 1945

Hiroshima was destroyed by the atom bomb on Aug. 5, 1945. The Japanese government surrendered unconditionally on Aug. 14. The efforts of THE TRIBUNE *were directed at once toward a peace of moderation and reconciliation.*

The peace upon which the world is entering presents mankind with what may well be its last opportunity to practice the virtues of fraternity and reason. All of us alike, the victors and the vanquished, are chained to this planet. If the old hates persist, if nations nurse their animosities and await the opportunity of vengeance, if men allow their minds to dwell upon the grievances of the long past, instead of turning with hope to the future, then it may yet be that this earth will become a barren waste, in which the survivors of the race will hide in caves or live among ruins.

The weapons whose awesome effects have now been demonstrated have transformed war from irrationality to idiocy, and these are only the beginning. The science of electronics is still in swaddling clothes. Neither a military occupation nor the policing of laboratory investigation can indefinitely withhold the discoveries already made by Americans from the scientists of nations which have gone down into defeat in

138

this war. Nor can any means of suppression be practiced which will insure that we, not they, will be first in achieving even more staggering advances.

The contemplation of such prospects imposes an obligation and responsibility upon the victors which will test their wisdom even more than their charitableness. Whether statesmen are capable of grasping how completely the world has changed within a very few days is still to be discovered. So far they have demonstrated little capacity to depart from traditional outlooks. The patchwork arrangements of the peace already made for Europe indicate, in fact, a retrogression into an older and more savage concept of the rights of victors. So far we have not utterly razed the cities of the defeated and sown the sites with salt, but the effect has been achieved in other ways.

One of the most discouraging aspects of the new, emerging world is that injustice has been crystalized by long practice in many parts of the globe. Liberty as Americans understand it is unknown in vast areas, and justice has no part in the intercourse of hundreds of millions of people. If tyrants can employ atomic power to perpetuate their sway over their cowed subjects, America may remain for generations an island of freedom in a slave world.

If the same power can be used by nations to dominate other nations, there will be no future for untold millions of persons, for there can be no hope. The subjected races will be helots in the service of the dominant. The notions of racial exclu-

siveness and superiority which characterized the mentality of Hitler will be perpetuated in other lands and by other men with no more compelling claim to moral worth than he. And these abhorrent doctrines will be reinforced by instruments capable of the total extinction of life as well as dissent.

But a world order resting upon such intolerable bases cannot last. It will only goad the victims to resistance and reprisal. Perhaps it might be many years before they could seize in their own hands the instruments of terror and death already held by their oppressors; but seize them, of a certainty, they finally will. A holocaust of unimaginable frightfulness would then be visited upon the world. Even if no nation could be the victor in this struggle, the just and the unjust, the enslaved and the enslavers, would go down together. It might easily be the end of civilization.

To avert such calamities the peacemakers must establish a rule of moderation and justice for the world. Toward this objective America can serve as a model. The bewildered and miserable people of a dozen prostrate lands would welcome our institutions and our liberties as eagerly as Americans received them in 1787 and in 1791, when the Bill of Rights was added to the original articles. Only tyrants, who live and retain power by means of fear and the perpetuation of ignorance, would oppose the establishment of a peace and a world dedicated to an enlargement of freedom.

It is the duty of America's leaders to assume the leadership in the serv-

139

ice of humankind that can come from nowhere else; to see that those justly condemned receive punishment; but to see likewise that all others are won to the common cause of a lasting peace, by endowing them with a stake in the future, with hope, with the right to life, liberty, and the pursuit of happiness. We can neither eradicate war by underwriting rearrangements of Europe's frayed fabric of power politics, nor by putting half the world on a permanent dole at American expense. Peace requires hope, and without freedom there is no hope.

THEIR FACES ARE RED

March 20, 1946

In this editorial much that was said earlier in THE TRIBUNE *in comment on the work of the various secret conferences is summarized. The disastrous consequences to be expected of the Potsdam agreements, for example, had been dealt with in three editorials published on Aug. 4, 1945.*

The hardest thing for the Roosevelt die-hards to take is the proof that he was the boob of the century.

His proved dishonesty does not bother them because they, too, are dishonest. That he let his country down has not affected them because they approved that and have continued the process of betrayal. But they thought he was supernaturally clever and they considered themselves, as his satellites, to be endowed with the same talent for manipulation with which they clothed the Roosevelt legend.

Mr. Roosevelt has been in his grave less than a year and already enough information has leaked out about his secret, ill conceived, disastrous deals in world statesmanship to demolish that legend for all time. Only Roosevelt, his sycophants insisted, had the profound knowledge of world affairs, the bold personality, and the diplomatic finesse to order the future of the world in the conferences with Churchill and Stalin.

The inside stories of those conferences are coming to light. They show that America got nothing out of them and Mr. Roosevelt got nothing except gratification of his ego. Mr. Churchill's recent fulminations in this country would indicate that he got nothing, altho he neglects to mention a few items of gain to the empire. Stalin, however, appears as the real slicker.

One of Mr. Roosevelt's own apologists and propagandists, Forrest Davis, confesses that at Tehran the President deliberately refrained from any show of firmness which might have alienated Stalin. Roosevelt sanctioned there the partition of Germany which gave Russia an excuse to devour, in exchange, a large portion of Poland.

It has come to light that when Secretary Hull took a stern view of the British-Russian agreement to divide the Balkans into spheres of influence, because it was a direct and flagrant violation of the Moscow agreement of 1943 to do away with spheres of influence, alliances, and power politics, he didn't know that Mr. Roosevelt had sanctioned the deal between Churchill and Stalin because Mr. Roosevelt hadn't bothered to tell his own secretary of state.

At Yalta, it has already been disclosed, Stalin was promised a substantial portion of Japanese territory, altho he did not go into the Japanese war until the enemy was about to surrender. It is beginning to appear, also, that he was promised extensive economic privileges in Manchuria at the expense of our absent ally, China.

Mr. Roosevelt's reward was Stalin's promise to support a new league of nations. Various reasons have been suggested for this faulty statecraft. They include his aristocratic pretensions and desire to ingratiate himself with the British nobility; his domestic political debts to the Communists who held the balance of political power in New York state; his failing health, which his own lieutenants described in the last year of his life as so bad that it was extremely difficult to get him to make a decision and even more difficult to make him stick to it; and, most probable of all, his supreme egotism, which led him to sacrifice every American interest toward the formation of a new league of nations which he hoped would set him down in history as the greatest statesman of all time.

It is not America alone that suffers from Mr. Roosevelt's incompetence in matters of diplomacy. His support of the insane Morgenthau plan and the dismemberment of Germany has, with the westward advance of Russia, which he also countenanced, reduced half of Europe to slavery and the other half to economic chaos. His sanction of the rape of Manchuria probably has deprived China of whatever chance it had of becoming a modern, industrialized nation. Only in Japan has the brilliant statesmanship of Gen. MacArthur been able to retrieve some of the Roosevelt errors. .

Mr. Roosevelt is shown to have been a plain boob, giving his confidence to Stalin, who was spying on him; posing as a great naval expert while bringing to this country the greatest naval disaster it ever experienced; and extracting allegiance to pious platitudes from his international confreres, who promptly ignored the platitudes to proceed with their imperialist programs. The Roosevelt die-hards may try to carry on their show in public, but in private their faces are very, very red.

SCORE OF THE WAR

May 17, 1946

At a time when many Americans, still under the influence of allied propaganda, were unaware of the extent of America's contribution to the victory, THE TRIBUNE *was determined to put the facts before the people. Other editorials stressed the statement of Gen. Eisenhower that America had far more soldiers on the fighting line in the climactic campaign in Europe than did Russia and nearly as many as all the allies together.*

The executive departments and agencies managed to withhold the figures showing comparative effort of the United States and its allies in the war until it was too late for Sen. Wheeler to use them personally in the debate on the British gift-

141

loan. These statistics, however, will and should have a tremendous effect on the consideration of the measure by the house.

The general picture shown by the figures is not new to the American people. They know already that our contribution was far greater than that of any of our allies, and in many respects greater than that of all of them together. What Mr. Wheeler has done, however, is to get together the most comprehensive and detailed presentation of these facts that the country has yet been privileged to see.

We did the most to win the war; we had less selfish reason to exert ourselves than any major ally; and for our sacrifices we have received little beyond insults and abuse. In the face of the figures no spokesman for Britain can ever again assert, if he values his reputation for telling the truth, that there was an inequality of sacrifice which left us in debt to the empire. Still less can the Russians, the French, the Chinese, or any minor ally expect to obtain credence for any such ridiculous claim.

These were our contributions to the common cause:

We spent more money to fight the war against Germany, Italy, and Japan than Russia and the British empire combined.

Our army and navy were the major force in the victory in Europe and almost the sole force in defeating Japan.

Our armies in Europe captured more German prisoners than the Russians, British, and French together.

Our war production was greater than the combined British and Russian output.

We equipped not only our own forces, but those of our allies. Lend-lease to the United Kingdom equaled one-third of that nation's own war expenditures. The Russian army could not have moved without our automotive equipment, to which we added billions of dollars' worth of guns, tanks and planes. The French [after 1942] and the Chinese got all their modern weapons from us.

We mobilized more men, out of a population of 140 million, than the British empire did from a population about four times as great.

Only in casualties was the American contribution exceeded, and our losses were low in comparison to what we accomplished because of superior American generalship and the superior training and equipment of our forces.

That is what we did. Why did we do it?

Once they were committed, there was no question as to why any of our major allies fought. They fought to save their necks. One of them was overwhelmed and the other three were so severely crippled that they would almost surely have succumbed without our help. But even today the American people are not certain why we entered the war or what national purpose was served by our entrance.

Britain and France had to fight Hitler because their bungling statesmen sat by for six years, during which they had the power to stop him, and let Hitler prepare a plan for world conquest. Once they were

142

in, they fought virtually the whole war with their backs to the wall. France crumbled, as much from internal rottenness as before German might.

The British were repeatedly routed on the battlefield and were harassed and killed in their homes. They were not fighting to keep Hitler from crossing the Atlantic; they were fighting to keep him from crossing the channel. The alternative for them was extinction as a nation and submission to nazi slavery. We applaud their courage in resisting, but we cannot concede that what they did was on our behalf.

Stalin launched Hitler against the western powers and split the booty of eastern Europe with him. When the nazi ally turned on the Russian accomplice the greater part of European Russia was overrun. It was only in the final months of the war, and only with the aid of billions of dollars' worth of American equipment, that the Russians were able to expel the Nazis from their homeland.

The Chinese had the best moral cause, one of outright aggression by Japan, but also the most feeble military effort. Our own efforts to help them were handicapped by Chinese venality and lack of patriotism as it exists in the western world.

Pearl Harbor was the climax of Roosevelt's program, not the beginning. We had been waging secret and unauthorized war against Germany for six months before. We went into this war to fight Hitler, not Japan, as Roosevelt's conduct of it demonstrates.

The best case that could be made

for our entry, and it is a woefully weak and hypocritical one, is that if Hitler had carried out his ambitious plan of conquest we in America would at some unstated time in the future have had to fight, without substantial allies, against a Europe organized for world conquest by the Germans.

At its strongest, this coalition would have consisted of a bruised and hated master race, less numerous than ourselves, and nations in chains and bitter against their masters. Our risk would have been that of attack on our fleets, the strongest in the world, by a naval conglomeration, half of which was not designed to fight on the ocean; by air forces, also heterogeneous and basically less efficient than ours proved to be; and by veteran nazi cadres stiffening disaffected levies from conquered peoples, the whole miscellaneous force compelled to seek our shores over 3,000 miles of turbulent ocean.

Our allies fought to save themselves and most Americans to this day cannot see why we fought except to save them.

These were the contributions and our reasons, such as they were, for making them. Look at the results.

Russia, whose perfidy launched the war, continues that perfidy to stifle the liberty of every nation that falls within the orbit of the might which we helped build.

Britain has become the most arrogant beggar in history, a people who, because we saved them, expect us to maintain them indefinitely.

The British, the French, the Dutch, whose liberty we saved,

143

abuse their own freedom by denying the most elementary political and economic rights to the slave populations of their colonial empires.

The imperial dominions, which we saved from invasion, deny us the bases we need to assure their safety as well as our own.

The hatreds of Europe, after a year of so-called peace, have inflicted famine on hundreds of millions of people. Americans are now depriving themselves of their own hard won resources to relieve this situation.

The center of appeasement has been transferred from Munich to Washington. Pusillanimous men with little minds, having already cost America more than a million casualties and burdened us with the greatest debt in history to achieve a victory by which we gained nothing, are continuing their efforts to bleed America white for the benefit of the greedy and ungrateful.

———

HOW TO MAKE A WAR

July 25, 1946

What was left unsaid as well as some of the things that were said in the Roberts report (Jan. 24, 1942) strengthened the growing conviction of the Editor that responsibility for the catastrophe at Pearl Harbor could not be confined to Gen. Short and Adm. Kimmel as official Washington wished the country to believe.

Thanks in great measure to the persistent campaign of THE TRIBUNE, *investigation succeeded investigation. The editorial which follows deals with the testimony assembled in the course of the congressional inquiry that produced the report of July 20, 1946.*

If there are any further doubts about how the country got into war, the Pearl Harbor reports will settle them.

By 1941 President Roosevelt had made up his mind to drag a reluctant people into war. In order to do so, he had to buck public opinion. The Gallup polls between October, 1939, and April, 1941, showed as high as 95 per cent, and never less than 83 per cent, of the people opposed to war.

"Peace and War," a state department review of foreign policy published in 1943, confesses that "during a large part of the period . . . much of public opinion did not accept the thesis that a European war could vitally affect the security of the United States." It adds, "Our foreign policy . . . had to move within the framework of a gradual evolution of public opinion in the United States away from the idea of 'neutrality' legislation." This legislation, it must be remembered, was sponsored by the Roosevelt administration and indorsed by the President himself, altho later deserted by him.

By April, 1941, Roosevelt's resolution to go to war had crystallized. He had a nondeclared war under way by then in the Atlantic against Germany and Italy. Beginning in January, and ending April 27, he had sent his military and naval representatives to a series of staff conferences in Washington and Singapore. At these meetings war plans were developed for combined American-British-Dutch operations against Japan if

Japanese forces started hostile action against British, Dutch, or American possessions or even against neutral Siam.

The President said nothing to congress or the people about this unlawful war alliance, but he approved the plans, "except officially," as was admitted by Adm. Stark, his chief of naval operations. Thereafter he and his principal Washington associates acted with the British and Dutch exactly as if a binding pact had been made. The Japanese also acted upon the same belief that the United States, Britain, and the Netherlands were working together, as, in fact, they were.

These were the sole war plans drafted for the Pacific. No separate over-all plan for the simple defense of American possessions against Japan was developed with any view of safeguarding American interests separately.

All thru this period Roosevelt was busy trying to sell war to the American people by dramatizing external threats. After the defeat of the luftwaffe attack upon Britain in the autumn of 1940, Hitler turned against Russia. He was in no mood to add to his problems by taking on the United States. He refused to permit Adm. Doenitz to mine Canadian waters or authorize U-boats to fight back when attacked by American destroyers. To have done so would have produced the incident that meant war.

Roosevelt unquestionably was looking for that incident. "The concept of an 'incident' as a factor which would unify public opinion behind an all out war effort either in the Atlantic or Pacific had influenced the thinking of officials for a long time," comments Rep. Keefe in the congressional reports.

Adm. Stark, discussing the garrisoning of Iceland with American marines in July, 1941, wrote Adm. Kimmel, "The Iceland situation may produce an 'incident.' Whether or not we will get an 'incident' ... I do not know—only Hitler can answer."

When a satisfactory incident was not forthcoming in the Atlantic, Roosevelt started looking for one in the Pacific. Under the axis pact of Sept. 27, 1940, Germany, Italy, and Japan agreed that a war involving the United States with any one of them would mean war with all three of them. If Germany wouldn't produce, maybe the Japanese would. "The question," said Secretary of War Stimson, "was how we should maneuver them into the position of firing the first shot without allowing too much danger to ourselves."

Roosevelt's first scheme was to station a patrol of American warships in two lines—Hawaii to the Philippines and Samoa to the Dutch Indies—to shut off all trade between Japan and North and South America. His naval commanders refused to accept responsibility. He then considered sending a detachment of warships to the far east and permitting a "leak" that they were going out there. As he told Stark, he would not mind losing one or two cruisers, but he did not want to take a chance of losing five or six.

He then thought of delivering a carrier load of aircraft to Russia via one of the Russian Asiatic ports. Adm. Kimmel, who would have been entrusted with this mission, said that to carry it out was "to invite war." He added, "If for any reasons of political expediency, it has been determined to force Japan to fire the first shot, let us choose a method which will be more advantageous to ourselves."

As late as Dec. 2, five days before Pearl Harbor, Roosevelt sent a direct order to Adm. Hart, commanding the Asiatic fleet, to charter three small vessels as a "defensive information patrol," qualify them as men of war by swearing in Filipino crews with naval ratings, installing an American naval officer in command of each, and mounting a small gun and a machine gun on them, and then send them into the Gulf of Siam in the path of a huge Japanese naval convoy. Had the Japanese fired on any of them it would have constituted an overt act, but Adm. Hart was unable to carry out his orders before Dec. 7.

As it turned out, Japan was maneuvered into firing the first shot at Pearl Harbor under stress of American diplomatic and economic pressure. Roosevelt then had his incident and his war, and a necessarily unified public support. Between his war mongering and the jingoism of the Jap militarists, the American people were helpless. They had war thrust upon them by the Rome-Berlin-Tokyo-Washington axis. They had no more voice in the decision than the helots of Hitler, Mussolini, Tojo, and Stalin.

It is a cynical distortion of history to say in the light of this record that an inevitable conflict was forced upon the "peace-loving" Mr. Roosevelt. He planned it that way, and if it hadn't happened at Pearl Harbor, it would have come somewhere else.

TO PHYLLIS WHO MIGHT SPELL IT PHREIGHT

August 7, 1946

THE TRIBUNE *for many years has been doing its part for spelling reform. Here the purpose and results of the campaign are outlined.*

A girl in the sixth grade named Phyllis who lives in California, wrote us a letter the other day, asking why we used the spelling *frate*. As a number of other readers have asked the same question, we publish our reply as the answer to all of them:

Dear Phyllis:

We think that the spelling of words in our language is very disorderly and we are trying to clean up the mess, a little at a time. That is why we have adopted simplified spellings of a few dozen words, including *frate*, in the hope that our readers, including the editors of other publications, will come to accept the changes.

If the changes annoy our readers too much, we go back to the old forms. The readers didn't like *iland* because they said it made them think of an African antelope; so we went back to *island*. *Frate* seems to be winning acceptance and we hear very few objections to *tho*, *thru*, *altho* and some others of the sort. Recently, we adopted *telegraf*, *geografy*, etc., but it is still too early to say how well or ill they have been received.

As you know, there is no official

spelling authority in this country. Spelling is a matter of custom; when you get 100 in spelling, you have spelled all your words the way they are customarily written in 1946, but that doesn't mean that the customary forms can't be improved. In fact, ever since there has been an English language, spelling has been changing and most of the changes have been simplifications. All we are trying to do is to carry along the work.

To show you that *frate* is not exactly a new spelling, and also to show you how much change has taken place in spelling in a few hundred years, we quote a sentence which we found in the Oxford English dictionary. It comes from Starkey's "England," published in 1538, and reads as follows:

"Specyally yf to that were joyned a nother ordynance . . . wych ys, concernyng the frate of marchandyse."

There is a very good chapter on spelling in the big book called "The American Language" by H. L. Mencken. In our copy, this chapter begins at page 379. You can find this book in almost any public library [but be sure to ask for "The American Language" and not for "The American Language: Supplement One" which is a wholly different book by the same author]. If you will read the chapter, you will find that the movement for simplified spelling had the approval of Benjamin Franklin, Theodore Roosevelt, and a lot of other distinguished men. You will learn, also, how much Noah Webster, the dictionary man, did to improve spelling when this country

was young. You will find that the same kind of people who today fuss about *frate* used to throw fits about *honor* and *labor*, which, they thought, must be spelled *honour* and *labour*. Maybe in a few years, people will think *freight* is a silly way to spell the word.

We hope this answers your question.

We may add that we are always glad to receive suggestions on spelling from readers. We can't promise to adopt all the proposals but we'll give them careful consideration.

VICTORY

November 7, 1946

For 14 years the New Deal controlled the White House and both houses of congress. On Nov. 5, 1946, the control of congress passed to the Republicans. The meaning of the election is appraised in this editorial.

Whatever doubts may have existed about the meaning of the huge registration have been removed. The people were aroused by manifest dangers to their country's future and to their own welfare. They won the greatest victory for the Republic since Appomattox.

The successful Republican candidates and party leaders deserve immense credit for the achievement, but in all truth it was not so much their doing as that of the voters themselves. The victory was not spotty: it was recorded in districts of weak as well as strong leadership. Across the continent, from coast to coast, the same story was repeated

147

—a truly awe inspiring testimony to the essential unity of the American people.

Those who passed Tribune Tower yesterday saw the building wearing its holiday dress of flags, with an especially large one flying at the top of the mast. This was done to express our view that the outcome of the election was not so much a partisan success as an American victory.

The meaning of the victory for this country is plain enough. The burocracy will be cut to size. Its arrogance will disappear and the conspiracy to destroy the economy of the country by meddling with it will be broken. The budget will be balanced and taxes will be reduced. The productive resources of the country will be stimulated. The era of shortages and standing in line is nearing its end.

The other nations do not yet understand the meaning of this election for them, and only here and there realize how much hope it brings to the world. America, the greatest and strongest of the nations, is the first one in the world in half a generation to turn its back definitely upon all forms of collectivism. There is no comfort in the news today for collectivists of any stripe, whether Socialists, Communists, or some other variety of totalitarian. This is a victory for free men in a free economy—the only kind of men and the only kind of economy that have ever given the world anything resembling political stability and plenty.

We have set the example here in America where it will count most heavily. We may look forward with some confidence to the gradual recovery of the great nations from the plague of governmental tyranny that has bedeviled men everywhere all these years.

The voters of America have rescued themselves and by doing so they will yet rescue the world. They have broken the evil combination that so long has held the government of this country captive—the combination of corrupt metropolitan machines with disloyal Communists and no less disloyal Anglomaniacs. Even the submerged peoples of southern Asia can rejoice, for now they know that the power of this country will not be dedicated to perpetual enslavement. Certainly no Republican elected to the house or senate need feel now that he is under any obligation to follow Mr. Truman in any further efforts along this line or, indeed, in any aspect of foreign policy that offends the conscience or injures the welfare of the American people.

———

SLAVEHOLDERS ALWAYS DEFEND SLAVERY

December 10, 1946

From the time the shooting ceased, THE TRIBUNE spoke for a humane peace. This is one of many editorials which have called for the liberation of prisoners, the return of loot, the withdrawal of the armies of occupation, and the restoration of civil government in enemy countries.

One fact thoroly proved by the history of human slavery is that the

148

slaveholder never lacks reasons, compelling to himself if to no one else, to hold on to his slaves.

For 50 years or more the grandfathers and great-grandfathers of President Truman, Secretary Byrnes and Sen. Connally shouted to the world their justifications for holding their black chattels. Slavery, they insisted, was ordained of God; it rescued Negroes from heathendom; it was the best possible way of life for the slave; it was the foundation of the country's economy. Reason could not prevail against these rationalizations.

It was expectable, therefore, that the French should advance all sorts of arguments for holding in indefinite slavery the 620,000 German prisoners of war whom the American army captured and turned over to the French. Ambassador Caffery's announcement in Paris the other day, that former President Bidault had given a qualified agreement to repatriate the prisoners, appears to have gone beyond the facts.

The French now assert that they are bound by no promises to release their slaves at any time. Byrnes and Truman, it appears, reverted to the practice of their forebears in a memorandum a year ago in which this precious pair agreed that the prisoners were to be chattels at forced labor as part of French reparations from Germany. The French say that Germany has no other way of paying reparations; that France has a great labor shortage; that it cannot maintain its economy without the slaves.

The French arguments are not merely immoral and disgraceful; they are irrelevant. Byrnes and Truman did not have the right to make their shameful gift; the French were without right to accept it. Both America and France are bound by the Geneva convention which forbids the enslaving of prisoners of war and provides that they must be repatriated at the end of the war. The shabby pretext that the war is still in progress cannot stand examination.

As for the contention that France has a labor shortage, what nation has not? We have one. Britain has one. Even nations like Sweden, which remained neutral during the war, are seeking labor abroad. There is a world shortage because of the necessity of repairing war damage and the war time wear on productive machinery, because of inflation, and because of pie in the sky demands by labor organizations, which all over the world are possessed by the delusion that men can live without working, or can live well by working only a little.

The French deepen their shame by aping Simon Legree in the abuse of their slaves. When slave miners struck recently, protesting that they were denied sufficient food to sustain heavy labor, and soap with which to keep clean, they were beaten and driven back to their tasks by Moroccan savages.

THE TRIBUNE'S was the first strong voice raised against the disgraceful revival of slavery in the post-war world. Others have joined us. The protests are beginning to have effect. We shall continue the fight until this terrible practice is stamped out.

149

And it will be stamped out. All of the decent people of the earth, in whatever country they live, stand with us. Their creed is Lincoln's—that those who would not be slaves, will not be slaveholders.

HAPPY NEW YEAR

January 1, 1947

For the hundredth time, THE TRIBUNE *extends the season's greetings to its readers.*

We wish all of our readers a happy New Year. May each of them pursue his happiness amid peace and plenty! In many lands overseas, 1947 will see a continuation of privation and strife, but in this most favored portion of this blessed land a happy New Year for the vast majority of us lies well within the bounds of possibility.

We are grateful for the many expressions of good-will we have been receiving of late. This is our hundredth New Year and we may be feeling a little sentimental on that account, but it seems to us that the good wishes this season have been more heartfelt than usual. If this is so, it is all the compensation we could ask for the years of anxiety thru which we have just passed; years when it would often have been much more comfortable to compromise principle than to adhere to it with steadfastness and candor.

We enter our centennial year knowing that devotion to the welfare of our community and our country has won us the confidence of a vast congregation of readers. They have made this a happy New Year for us; we shall continue to do all in our power to make it a happy one for them.

INDEX

Abolition of slavery, 12-13
Administration, illegal conduct before
Pearl Harbor, 137
Advertising in Tribune, statistics for
Jan. 2-May 15, 1881 (table), 61
Aero Club of America, 81
"Age of iron," 52-54
Air power, importance of, in war with
Japan, 131-32;
of United States, in World War I, 81-82
Alliances, entangling, avoided by United
States, 59-60
Altgeld, John P., 61
Amendments, see Constitution
Anarchists, and Haymarket riot, 61-63
Anthracite strike of 1902, 71-73
Archbold, John D., 77
Army of United States, First division, in
World War I, 86-87
Atlantic conference, 1941, 129-30
Atomic warfare, 138-39
Austin, Warren, 134

Balkans, British-Russian agreement on,
140-41
Banking crisis, Roosevelt's handling of,
108-109
Bermudas, 60
Bernstorff, Count von, 80
Black, Hugo, appointed Supreme Court
judge, 119
Black laws of Illinois, 17
Boom of 1879, 52-54
Bossism, 77
Boycott of Japan, 120
Brewing industry, and political corrup-
tion, 87-88
Brice, Calvin Stewart, 69
British Guiana-Venezuela boundary
dispute, 64-66
British navy, 60
Brown, John, 12-13
Bryan, William Jennings, and Scopes
trial, 95-97
Buchanan, James, 10, 11, 19
Bulloch, James, 129

Burgess, William, 76
Burlington strike of 1888, 72
Byrnes, James F., 149

California, elects Woodrow Wilson, 83-84;
hatred of Japanese, 83-84
Canada, 59
Canadian reciprocity agreement, 73-74
Cannon, Joseph G., 74
Capital and labor, 71-73
Carnegie, Andrew, 93
Carnegie strike of 1892, 72
Censorship of press, 105
Chandler, Zachariah, 56
Chicago, political corruption during
Thompson regime, 93-95
Chicago fire, 41-42
Chicago Times, see Times, Chicago
Chicago Tribune, see Tribune
Churchill, Winston, and Atlantic con-
ference with Roosevelt, 129-30;
and Russian aggression, 127-28;
conferences with Roosevelt, 140-41
Circulation of Tribune, statistics for
Jan. 2-May 15, 1881 (table), 61
Civil liberty, 39-41
Civil service reform, 49-50
Clark, Grenville, 134
Cleveland, Grover, message on British
Guiana-Venezuela boundary dispute,
64-66;
opens Chicago World's Fair, 63
Columbian exposition in Chicago, 1893,
63-64
Communism, 110
Communist movement in America, 42-43
Confederacy, 20
Conscription, 134-135
Conspiracy laws, 62-63
Constitution, 16th amendment, 82;
18th amendment, 87-88, 98;
19th amendment, 35-37;
21st amendment, 107-108
Cooke, Jay, 50
Copperheads, 33
Covode, John, 19

151

INDEX

INDEX

Hitt, Robert R., 7
Hoare, Sir Samuel, 116
Homestead strike of 1892, 72
Hughes, Charles Evans, 105
Hull, Cordell, 140

Illinois, legislature, corrupt practices in Lorimer affair, 74-76
Illinois, slavery in, 3-4
Incandescent lamp, invented by Edison, 54-56
Income taxes, 82-83
India, 60
Indian lands, sale of, 34-35
Insull, Samuel, 100
International treaties, sanctity of, 119-21. See also Versailles treaty
Intervention, American, in foreign wars, 119-21, 125-26
Ireland, 59
Irish Free State, 117
Iron industry, 52-54. See also Steel industry
Isolationism of United States, 58-60

Jackson, Justice, on Nuernberg trials, 137-38
Japan, boycott of, 120; joins Axis, 125-26
Japanese in California, 83-84
Johnson, Andrew, impeachment trial, 30-34; stand of Republican senators, 31-34
Johnson, Hugh, 113, 114

Kansas-Nebraska bill, 6
Kellogg-Briand outlawry of war pact, 119, 137
Ku Klux Klan, 39, 119

Labor, and capital, 71-73; draft of, during war time, 133-35
Lemmon case, 4
Lincoln, Abraham, assassination, 29-30; Emancipation Proclamation, 26-27; eulogies by *Tribune*, 11-12, 14-15; nomination to presidency, 14-17; profile of, in 1860, 18-19;

stand on emancipation, 24; "strong man," 56
Lincoln-Douglas debates, 4-5
Lincoln-Douglas senatorial race, Horace Greeley's stand, 10-11; Lincoln defeated, 11-12; *Press and Tribune* appeals to voters, 8-9
Liquor traffic, 87-88, 107-108
Lodge, Henry Cabot, 69
Lorimer, William, 74-76
Lundin-Thompson regime in Chicago, 95
Lusitania, sinking of, 80

Maine, battleship, sinking of, 66, 67
McAdoo, William G., 82
MacArthur, Douglas, 141; qualities of leadership, 132-33
McKinley, William, 66-68
Marx, Karl, 42
Medill, Joseph, resumes control of *Tribune*, 43-46
Military bases, leased to United States by Great Britain, 124-25
Military rule in 1871, 39-41
Militia, 134
Minnesota gag law, 103-105
Missouri Compromise, 6
Mitchell, John, 71
Monroe Doctrine, 64-66
Most, Johann Joseph, 61
Mussolini, Benito, 116

NRA code for newspapers, 113; government attempt to get *Tribune* to accept code, 115-16
Nationalism in America, 81
Naval power, *versus* air power, 131-32
Nazi trials at Nuernberg, 137-38
Nazis in Germany, 109-10
Near, J. M., 103
New Deal, 111-12
Newspapers, see Press
Nine power treaty for protection of China, 119, 120
Nineteenth amendment, see Constitution
Nineteenth century, achievements of, 70-71

153

INDEX

Northern Pacific railroad, 50

Office-seeking, 49-50
Office-Tenure law, 31, 32
Oglesby, Richard J., 61
Olney, Richard T., 65
Opium trade in China, 59

Pacifist movement, 91
Panic of 1873, causes, 50-52
Paris Commune, 42, 43
Paternal government, 37-39
Patronage in federal service, 49-50
"Peace and War," state department review
  of foreign policy, 1943, 144
Peace of future, America to assume leader-
  ship in, 139-40
Pearl Harbor disaster, Dec. 7, 1941, 130-
  31; investigations, 144-46
Pendleton, George Hunt, 33
Pershing, John J., 86-87
Philippines, air war over, forecast by
  Tribune, 131-32;
  independence, 89-90;
  prediction of capture, 90;
  strategic weakness, 89-91
Pittsburgh, steel center, 93
"Pittsburgh plus" freight rates, abolished,
  92-94
Potsdam agreement, 140
Presidential election, of 1876, contested,
  46-49;
  of 1880, "strong man" cry, 56-58
Presidency, third term tradition, 56, 123-
  124
Press, censorship of, 105;
  duty in time of war, 22-24;
  freedom of, *see* Freedom of press;
  relations to political parties, 45-46;
  unanimity on anthracite strike of 1902,
  71-72
Press and Tribune, appeals to voters in
  Lincoln-Douglas senatorial race, 8-9;
  eulogizes Lincoln, 11-12, 14-15;
  last entreaty to nominate Lincoln for
  presidency, 16-17;

reporting of Lincoln and Douglas
  speeches, 6-8;
  word to campaign subscribers, 9-10
Prisoners of war, from World War II,
  liberation advocated by *Tribune*, 148-50
Prize fighting, legalized, in Illinois, 85-86
Progressive party, 77
Prohibition, and 18th amendment, 87-88;
  repeal, and 21st amendment, 107-108;
  Tribune stand on, 97-99, 107-108
Prosperity in United States in 1879 and
  years following, 52-54, 58-60
Pullman strike in 1894, 72

Railroads and panic of 1873, 50-52
Raulston, Judge and Scopes trial, 95-97
Ray, C. H., 44
Reciprocal trade agreements, 73-74
Red tape in United States government, 115-16
Refugees, find haven in United States, 59
Religious toleration, 39
Republican government, 37
Republican party, and trusts, 68-70;
  composition, 45-46;
  Tribune, an independent Republican
  journal, 44-46;
  victory at polls on Nov. 5, 1946, 147-48
Republican party of Illinois, platform
  adopted in 1858, 5
Roadhouses, 88
Roosevelt, Franklin Delano, and Atlantic
  conference, 1941, 129-30;
  and freedom of press, 113, 114;
  and future of Supreme Court, 117-19;
  and government spending, 106-107;
  and third term tradition, 123-24;
  and Wilson slogan "He kept us out of
  war," 119-21;
  commits America to war, 129-30;
  conferences with Churchill and Stalin,
  140-141;
  forces issue of war with Japan, 125-26;
  foreign policy, 119-21;
  handling of banking crisis, 108-109;
  dedicates Outer Drive bridge of Chicago,
  119-21;

154

INDEX

INDEX

and freedom of press, 94-95, 103-105, 113-14;
challenges legality of Nuernberg and Tokyo trials, 137-38;
circulation from Jan. 2 to May 15, 1881 (table), 61;
Dr. Evans "How to Keep Well," 78;
efforts to defeat William Hale Thompson, 103;
exposes bribery in Lorimer case, 74-76;
"fault is to be in advance of public opinion," 24-26;
forecast "If Russia Wins," 126-28;
forecast of air war over Philippines, 131-32;
independence of seaboard leadership, 10-11;
independent Republican journal, 44-46;
Joseph Medill resumes control, 43-46;
libel suit brought by Mayor Thompson, 93-95;
poll on reciprocity, June 3, 1911, 73-74;
stand on prohibition, 97-99; and growth in circulation, 98-99;
statistics of advertising, Jan. 2-May 15, 1881 (table), 61;
"World's Greatest Newspaper," 60-61
Truman, Harry, 149
Trusts, as political issue, 68-70;
steel trust and "Pittsburgh Plus" freight rates, 93, 94
Twentieth century, prophecies for, 70, 71
Twenty-first amendment, see Constitution
Twiggs, David Emanuel, 22
Two-party system, 45

Union, restoration of, after Civil War, 27-29
United States, contribution to World War II, 141-44;
entry into World War II, 144-46;
government tries to make deal with *Tribune*, 115-16;
intervention in World War I, 80-81;
"our country's future," after Civil War, 27-29;

unpreparedness at outset of World War I, 81-82
United States Steel corporation, 92-93

Venezuela-British Guiana boundary dispute, 64-66
Versailles treaty, 88-89;
and Nazi Germany, 110
Volstead act, 98

Washington disarmament conference, 91
Wealth, taxation of, 82-83
Wendell, Cornelius, 19
West Indies, 59
White, Charles A., 75
White, Horace, 44
White man's burden, to be shared by America, 58-60
Whitney, William C., 69
Wilson, Woodrow, and Versailles treaty, 88-89;
election, 77;
foreign policy, 119-21;
reelection, 83;
slogan "He kept us out of war," 119-21
Women's rights, 35-37
World War I, American intervention, 80-81;
First division of American army, 86-87;
lack of preparedness of United States, 81-82;
twilight of kings, 78-79;
Versailles treaty, 88-89
World War II, America's contribution, 141-44;
forecast of Japanese strategy, 89-91;
prophetic cartoon in *London Herald*, 1919, 122;
United States entry into, 144-46;
war the world feared, 121-23
World's Fair at Chicago, 1893, 63-64
Wright, Hendrick B., 54

Yalta conference, 141

156